Praise for Chris Townsend

'I was struck by his ~~373~~ ~~732~~ ~~Drymen~~ ness and clear-sighted if during endless ho ile alone on the trail.'

Scotsman

'In the Scottish ou shine like the stars and very quickly fade into the night Townsend has remained a shining light for well over 35 years, a passionate and inspiring advocate for the wild corners of our land, an enthusiast who literally walks the walk.'

Cameron McNeish

'Chris Townsend is the all-around world champion hiking memoirist, guide, photographer, blogger, and techie.'

Ron Strickland, founder of the Pacific Northwest Trail

'I first met Chris Townsend about thirty years ago cross-country skiing in the Cairngorms. He is someone who practices what he preaches. I have much appreciated his insights and knowledge and he is a great voice for our cause.'

Peter Pearson, Chair of the John Muir Trust

Praise for *Out There*

'Townsend has achieved his aim of inspiring others with this book and if you don't feel like going on a walk – no matter how long or short – after reading it, you never will.'

The Scots Magazine

'*Out There* is not just a wonderfully written celebration of backpacking and mountaineering. It's also a call to arms – a warning that nobody but us will step in to save the wild places we love, and that we all have a responsibility to protect and nurture the environment.'

Alex Roddie

'What shines through this highly readable anthology is the author's passionate plea for the protection of our wild country.'

Outdoor Focus

'Those making the decisions about what happens to wild land would do well to listen to people like Townsend who really understand wild places not for what they are, but for what they can offer.'

Active Outdoors

'Ranging from the Pacific Crest Trail to the Sierras to the peaks of Britain, *Out There* is a collection of essays from the many walks of his own life. Brought together, they read as a singular celebration of wild spaces.'

Geographical Magazine

'Chris is a compelling and engaging author . . . too many delights in its pages to describe in a brief review, I suggest you read and enjoy it.'

Beryl Leatherland, *Wild Land News*

Chris Townsend is possibly the world's most experienced long-distance walker who also writes. He is the author of many books including *Grizzly Bears and Razor Clams*, his account of the Pacific Northwest Trail, *Rattlesnakes and Bald Eagles*, his account of the Pacific Crest Trail, and *Out There*, which won the Outdoor Writers and Photographers Guild Outdoor Book of the Year Award in 2016. All were published by Sandstone Press. He is gear correspondent for *The Great Outdoors* magazine and has a website as Chris Townsend Outdoors where his popular blog receives many thousands of visitors.

ALONG THE DIVIDE

WALKING THE WILD SPINE
OF SCOTLAND

Chris Townsend

SANDSTONE PRESS

First published in Great Britain in 2018
Sandstone Press Ltd
Dochcarty Road
Dingwall
Ross-shire
IV15 9UG
Scotland.

www.sandstonepress.com

Editor: Robert Davidson

The publisher acknowledges support from Creative
Scotland towards publication of this volume.

ISBN: 978-1-912240-22-7
ISBNe: 978-1-912240-23-4

Cover and plate sections designed by Raspberry Creative Type, Edinburgh
Typography by Biblichor Ltd, Edinburgh
Printed and bound by CPI Group (UK) Ltd, Croydon, CR0 4YY

To Denise

CONTENTS

ACKNOWLEDGEMENTS

Peter Wright for inspiring the walk, for all his work on protecting the Watershed, and for his company at the start and finish.

All the people I met along the way for their friendship and interesting conversation and when needed their help.

My partner, Denise Thorn, who, as always, listened patiently to me talking about the book time and time again and who read through the text making many corrections and useful suggestions.

Robert Davidson of Sandstone Press for his help, encouragement and patience.

Heather Macpherson for the cover and the design.

Helen Stirling for the maps.

LIST OF MAPS

LIST OF ILLUSTRATIONS

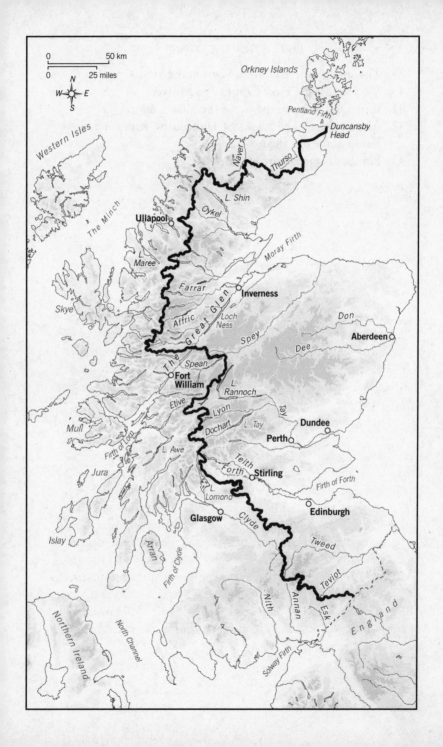

1

BEGINNINGS

A watershed, a divide, between two worlds. A raindrop falls, a bog oozes, a trickle begins, running gently downhill, eventually to reach the ocean. Not far away there's a repeat, in the other direction, maybe heading for a different ocean. Watersheds are significant, dividing the land. Significant enough for us to use them as metaphors for sudden changes in life. 'A watershed moment', we say: a moment when something could go either way, in our personal lives, in national or world affairs, with the suggestion that once it happens it cannot be changed, much as the water running downhill can never go the other way.

A watershed is a line that links continuous high ground. Watersheds can be small, just the ridge between two valleys, or can run the length of countries. In Scotland the main Watershed is between the Atlantic Ocean and the North Sea. It's not a straight line though, far from it. It twists and turns, sometimes heading in what seem perverse directions. Following the Watershed north you can at times find yourself heading south. Scotland is roughly 410 km from south to north. The Watershed covers three times that distance, some 1,200 km. On its journey it crosses the major regions of the Scottish landscape – the Southern Uplands, Central Lowlands, Highlands and the Flow Country. Because Scotland has an overall tilt from west to east the Watershed is mostly towards the west side of the country rather than down the centre, though there are a few wanderings eastwards.

For most of its length the line, convoluted though it may be, is clear. Water either ends up running west into the Atlantic Ocean or east into the North Sea. However, Scotland has a north coast as well as west and east ones. Where is the Watershed there? This is debatable. Peter Wright in *Ribbon of Wildness: Discovering the Watershed of Scotland* argues it runs to Duncansby Head, the north-eastern point of the mainland, as the Pentland Firth just to the north is where the North Sea meets the Atlantic Ocean. Rivers run north to the latter here, and south-east to the former. You can see the line between these rivers clearly on the map. Follow it exactly on the ground and you'll cross no running water. David Edgar, who set out to walk the Watershed of Scotland and England and whom I was to meet on my walk, chose Dunnet Head, the most northerly point on the mainland, as the National Hydrographic Organisation says this is where the Atlantic meets the North Sea. Dave Hewitt walked the Scottish Watershed in one continuous journey in 1987, a significant adventure described in his excellent book *Walking the Watershed: The Border to Cape Wrath along Scotland's Great Divide* (available online at http://gdl.cdlr.strath.ac.uk/hewwat/), and he reckons anywhere on the north coast will do as the east-west Watershed finishes further south. Resisting the appeal of finishing over the mountains at Cape Wrath I decided that Peter Wright's view made most sense, even though it meant walking across the boggy Flow Country.

The Watershed isn't a geographical feature that received much attention until *Ribbon of Wildness, Discovering the Watershed of Scotland* came out in 2010 and Peter Wright began his enthusiastic and indefatigable campaign to promote its conservation. Before then it was little known though a few walkers had explored it. Mike Allen and Malcolm Wylie had separately walked the whole watershed of mainland Britain in a series of short trips while Martin Prouse walked the Scottish Watershed from Rowardennan to Ben Hope. The only book I knew about it was *Walking the Watershed* which I read and enjoyed when it was published. I became engrossed in Hewitt's adventure, but I didn't gain much of an impression of the Watershed from it. That came much later when I read Wright's book, which is much more a description of the Watershed rather than the story of an adventure (Wright walked the route in a series of journeys). In fact, so little did I grasp the significance of the Watershed that when I wrote a guide to the Scottish hills (*Scotland World Mountain Ranges*) I didn't mention it, an omission that seems astonishing to me now, though I did list Hewitt's book in the bibliography. Since *Ribbon of Wildness* was published two runners have done the Watershed, Colin Meek and Elspeth Luke, which is really impressive given how tough some of the terrain is even for walking.

When I read *Ribbon of Wildness* the idea of a continuous line of wild land stretching through Scotland really sank in and I felt excited and enthused. Walking the Watershed suddenly became something I wanted to do, to see what it was like, to revel in its wildness (hopefully!), and to spend weeks in natural surroundings, camping at night, walking during the day. I would go for the experience, for an unbroken journey, for the joy of being in the wilds for weeks at a time.

This wasn't the first time the desire to do a long walk had been inspired by a book. Most of my long walks have been. Reading, as well as long-distance walking, is a passion of mine. The words on the page set thoughts racing through my head, make me want to be there, make me want to experience the reality of what the author is describing. When reading *Ribbon of Wildness* what evoked these feelings was the real-isation of how varied the Watershed was and what a long-distance route it could make. I felt that familiar tingle that meant I really wanted to do this walk, to find out what the Watershed had to offer. It almost felt as though this was something I'd been waiting to discover, especially now that I lived in Scotland, having moved from England nearly a quar-ter of a century ago. It was an opportunity to walk the country from end to end. I had undertaken two long walks in Scotland before. One, a decade before I moved here, was part of my first-ever long-distance walk, from Land's End to John O'Groats. The other was a round of the Munros and Tops six years after I moved. On neither of these had I been thinking about Scotland itself. Now firmly my home and committed to the country, a Watershed walk would be very different. I saw it as an opportunity to see how the country is connected, how the different parts fit together. And how I felt about it.

It also wasn't the first time I'd followed a watershed. Twenty-eight years before this walk I'd hiked the Continental Divide Trail, over 4,800 km from Canada to Mexico down the watershed of the USA. On that walk I'd learnt how following a watershed is an excellent way to see a country unfold before you. One place epitomised the Divide for me and really showed just what a country-long watershed is. In the Teton Wilderness in the Rocky Mountains in Wyoming I came to a sign marking the Parting of the Waters where North Two Ocean Creek splits into two little trickling streams, one start-ing a 5,613-km journey to the Atlantic Ocean, the other heading 2,177 km to the Pacific. There are places on the Scottish Watershed where it is narrow, and you can see water destined for the North Sea on one side and the Atlantic Ocean on the other. I'd been to some of these already but had never realised I was on the Watershed. I was looking forward to returning and seeing the landscape in a different way.

Since moving to Scotland I'd become increasingly concerned about the conservation of nature and wild land and become involved with the conservation movement in Scotland, initially for the Mountaineering Council of Scotland (now Mountaineering Scotland), and, since the walk, the John Muir Trust. Just how wild and unspoilt would Scotland feel if I walked it from one end to the other on the Watershed? What was the potential for Peter Wright's 'ribbon of wildness' to really mean something? Years of looking at wild places, here and abroad, and reading natural history and conservation books meant I knew that nature in Scotland was in a poor condition in too many places. Overgrazing, forestry plantations, industrial developments and more had led to a degraded landscape with poor biodiversity. Once seen and understood this was hard to ignore. American conservationist Aldo Leopold wrote in his seminal book *A Sand County Almanac*, 'One of the penalties of an ecological education is that one lives alone in a world of wounds. Much of the damage inflicted on land is quite invisible to laymen.' Walking down a treeless glen with little wildlife I know exactly what he meant. Maybe I would find a Watershed walk made me sad at what has been lost. At the same time, I knew of all the organisations working on protection and restoration, giving hope that there is a positive future for nature and wildness. Maybe I would see enough to feel optimistic.

I was aware too of the wonderfully named, but really rather sad, idea of 'shifting baseline syndrome' by which each generation assumes that the current state of nature is the norm. This can lead to people protecting damaged land rather than trying to restore it or even trying to recreate a damaged landscape. Reading accounts of what forests and wildlife were like in earlier centuries, and of the effects of the Clearances and the Coming of the Sheep and then the deer stalking and grouse shooting estates, made me realise that very little of even the best of what I would see on the Watershed would be near what it could be. It was from such reading that I knew how empty and bare too many glens are of people and wildlife, knowledge reinforced by walking overseas in places where nature was much healthier. From a Watershed walk I hoped to gain a bigger overall picture of what was happening. A ribbon of wildness the length of the country would be a big step towards ecological restoration on a landscape scale.

However, despite my awareness of the state of wild land and nature in Scotland, I did expect to enjoy the walk. I wasn't setting out to have a miserable time. As walking in wild places is my passion, especially for weeks at a time, I expected to mostly feel content and satisfied. Just being out in nature walking and camping every day is enough to lighten my spirits. I hoped for surprises along the way too, surprises that would please and cheer me, wildlife in unexpected places, beautiful light, calmness and peace. I also knew that even when damaged, nature always has something to offer. As the cliché goes: as long as there is life there is hope. Overgrazed land can recover, plantations can turn into more natural forests, wildlife can return. This is the process now known as rewilding. It needs to happen, and on a large scale. The Watershed could be part of this, a corridor linking areas of wild land, a corridor along which species could travel to new areas.

Much of Scotland is scenically beautiful, grand and spectacular despite the ecological deficit. Except in places where the latter really impinged on my consciousness, I was looking forward to spending so much time in the wilds of the

Southern Uplands and the Highlands (though I wasn't so sure about the Central Lowlands). Being in wild places I always find uplifting. There's no real wilderness in Scotland, of course. Nearly everywhere has been touched by humanity. But land can still be wild and show little visible sign of people's influence. Scottish Natural Heritage says wild land consists of 'largely semi-natural landscapes that show minimal signs of human influence'. I hoped and expected to see much of that on the Watershed.

I love walking as a way to see places properly, to see details and subtlety missed at faster speeds, and I love long-distance walking the most because there is time to immerse myself into nature and wild places, time to really feel part of a place. Moving on day after day is also a way to see how the land changes, how changes in the underlying rocks alter landforms, sometimes gradually, sometimes abruptly. As a walk progresses I gain an overall feel for the whole route, for how it's all linked. This is helped if I have some understanding of how the landscape came to be the way it is. Knowing a little about the geology and geomorphology of the places I walk through adds greatly to my enjoyment, just as being able to identify wildlife and trees and plants does.

As well as the natural history I also like to learn about the human history. The Watershed has few habitations and only one town but there are many signs of human presence and activity going back to Roman times and earlier. I was interested to see just how much remained and how easy it was to understand. The Watershed today is very much what people have made of it, even if that's only a fence marking an estate boundary.

The effects of long walks can take time to surface. No long walk is ever exactly as expected, at least not for me. It would

7

be boring if one was. During a walk my thoughts and feelings about it develop and change. They continue to do so afterwards, for weeks, months, years. At the same time as I undertook this walk I was also thinking deeply, though often not clearly, about living in Scotland, where I'd moved twenty-four years earlier. This was now my country but what did that mean? How had I changed in that time? Walking the length of the country, and the aftermath of the walk, would stimulate thoughts and feelings that would surprise and disturb me.

The Watershed was not a walk I expected to be easy. There's no path most of the way – people cross the Watershed, not go along it – and the terrain can be boggy and rough. There are no signposts either. In fact, there are no mentions of the Watershed anywhere along it. The average height is 450 metres but is higher than that through most of the Southern Uplands and the Highlands. If the weather was stormy the wind and rain would be stronger and heavier on the highest ground.

The Watershed runs over forty-four Munros (mountains over 3,000 feet/914.4 metres) and twenty-four Corbetts (between 2,500 feet/762 metres and 3,000 feet/914.4 metres) – the lists were compiled before metric heights were used in Scotland), the highest being 3,776 foot/1,151 metre- Sgurr nan Ceathreamhan, whose name, appropriately, means hill of the quarters, referring to land division. The low point on the Watershed is just 35 metres above sea level at Laggan in the Great Glen, not, as you might expect, at Duncansby Head, where the top of the cliffs is 60 metres above the sea, or somewhere in the Central Lowlands. The Great Glen is narrow and the Watershed spends very little time so low down.

Resupplying is difficult too, especially north of the Great Glen where there were no towns or villages near the Watershed.

Actually on the Watershed there is only one town, Cumbernauld in the Central Lowlands. Leaving the route would be necessary for every other resupply, sometimes going quite a distance. That's always a dilemma on a long-distance walk. Carry more weight in supplies and stay on the route longer or leave it more frequently to resupply but carry less so you can do more miles a day without getting tired. From previous walks I knew that once I was carrying more than ten days' food my pack would feel really heavy, so I planned on never needing that much.

The Watershed isn't marked on maps and there's no guide-book either, though *Ribbon of Wildness* gives a fairly detailed description of the route. Using that book, I drew the Watershed on the relevant Ordnance Survey maps, twenty-two in all. These I'd send to myself at Post Offices in places where I was planning on resupplying. I also had *Ribbon of Wildness* on my e-reader. In my journal, a small notebook with waterproof covers as usual, I wrote the names of supply points and the estimated dates of arrival. After that I just had to try and stay fit before I set out, not usually an easy task as there's always masses of deskwork to catch up with before leaving it behind for a few months.

When undertaking a long walk, I think of it in stages as the final destination always seems too far away in distance and time to be real. Walking 1,000 km sounds much more difficult than walking 100 km ten times. Each section seems feasible. Complete them all and there's the whole walk.

The Watershed breaks conveniently into five sections, four of them determined by significant and clearly visible geological features – the Southern Upland Fault, Highland Boundary Fault, and Great Glen are long straight lines cutting right across the country. Peter Wright calls each of these sections a march, meaning a boundary or border (from a Scots word derived from the Anglo-Saxon 'mearc'), a term still used in the Borders. This is appropriate as the Watershed has been a boundary for centuries with many estates, parishes, councils and more using it as such. Today around 70 per cent of the Watershed still forms the boundary between estates. In many places, especially in the Southern Uplands, a fence or wall marks the boundary and thus the line of the Watershed. As Peter Wright says, communities tended to look downhill, away from the highest ground. The Watershed forms a natural boundary.

Heading north, the direction I'd decided to walk, the first section is the Southern Uplands, the Reiver March, named for the border raiders and cattle thieves once notorious here. The hills run east-west here, and the Watershed follows them at first so starts off westwards. These are big rounded grass and heather hills, many heavily sheep-cropped, others covered with commercial forestry plantations. There is little natural forest. The underlying rock is sedimentary – sandstones and shales – and there are few crags. Although the terrain on the tops can make for easy walking the slopes are often steep and the Watershed makes no concession to this, going straight up and down. I'd walked through these hills twice on the coast-to-coast Southern Upland Way so knew what they were like. The Watershed is higher than that trail though, with an average height of 550 metres and a high point of 808 metres on Hart Fell. This section ends after 133 km at the Southern Upland Fault where the hills simply stop and you look across the gently undulating expanse of the Central Lowlands.

Peter Wright names the Central Lowlands, the Laich March, from the Scots word for low, and, as you'd expect, the Watershed is lower here than in other sections. It still has an average height of 280 metres. Linking many small hill ranges the Watershed takes quite a convoluted line, winding its way 175 km first east and then west. This wasn't an area I knew well, and it was one I hoped would surprise me by being wilder and less developed than I suspected despite all the roads and towns.

To the north of the Central Lowlands the Highlands can often be seen, tempting you onwards. These are divided by the Great Glen, and Peter Wright splits them into two Marches, the Heartland and the Moine. The first has the highest average elevation at 610 metres of all the sections and is 240 km long. The Highland Boundary Fault can be clearly seen as you climb out of the Central Lowlands. Across the Great Glen the Moine March, named for the Moine Thrust, a key geological feature that lies just west of the Watershed, has an only slightly lower average height of 595 metres and is the longest section at 330 km. These sections, making up around half of the Watershed, are the ones I knew best, the ones with all the Munros, which I'd climbed several times. Looking at the maps I realised there were still long unfamiliar stretches. The Watershed doesn't coincide with that many routes up the hills. The terrain is mostly steep and rugged so the going on the Watershed looked tough.

Where the Watershed turns north-east and starts its final journey to Duncansby Head it leaves the Highlands for the Flow Country, Peter Wright's Northland March. This was the area I knew least, never having walked here. Its reputation for soft boggy ground that was difficult to cross concerned me a little. Around 180 km of mostly peatbogs didn't appeal. With an average elevation of 240 metres the Watershed in the Flow Country is even lower than in the Central Lowlands.

These five sections are obvious, logical and appealing and I did come to view the Watershed like this. They weren't ideal for planning though as there weren't convenient places to resupply near the Watershed at the start and finish of each one. Four resupply points wasn't enough anyway, unless I wanted to carry really heavy loads. I wrote down eleven possibilities in my notebook. I'd end up using eight of them.

Planning and research finished. Maps posted, rucksack packed. Now there was just the walk. The Watershed awaited.

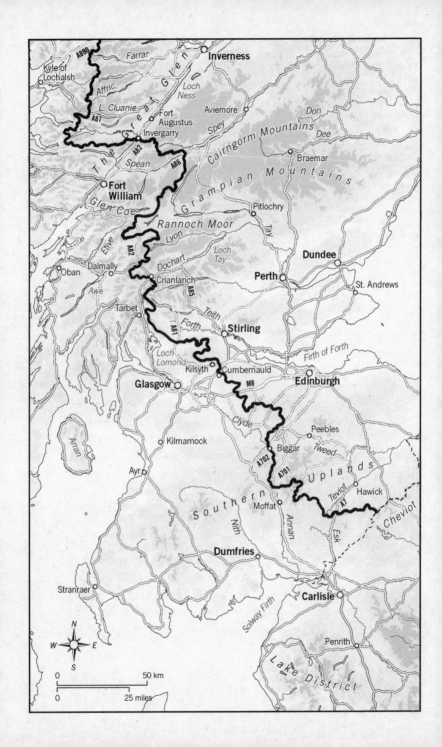

2

ALONG THE SOUTHERN UPLANDS

'He said you can't camp up there without permission, so I said we'll nip across the border'. Peter Wright had just returned from arranging to leave his car at the Kielder Camp Site in Northumberland. A difference between Scotland and England had surfaced right at the start of the walk, reminding me that I was in a different country now. Permission to camp was not something that would come up again due to Scotland's access rights, which include the right to wild camp. There is no such right in England.

We didn't cross the border before camping, so my first night on the Scottish Watershed walk was in England and was technically illegal. Given that we were camped in mist in a bog I wasn't concerned anyone would notice. We'd climbed through the dark and dense conifers of the Kielder Forest onto the slopes of Deadwater Fell and camped out of sight of the summit with its large radar station, not far from the border and the start of the Watershed.

The first night was stormy with strong gusty winds and heavy showers. The temperature dropped near to freezing despite it being late May. I slept fitfully, which I put down to the bumpy site and the wind and rain rattling my shelter. There was probably some excitement, anticipation and trepidation mixed in too, as usual at the start of a long-distance walk. The planning was over, the journey had begun. I was committed now to whatever lay ahead.

Peter's plan was to accompany me to the top of Peel Fell where he would show me the Watershed stretching over the hills. The first part of this was fine and Peter slogged over the boggy ground to the summit with me. The weather put a stop to the second part though. We were in dense mist and could see barely 10 metres. After the obligatory photos Peter departed. I wouldn't see him again for fifty-five days and that would be at the far end of the country. I was glad he'd come to Peel Fell with me. I'd not had anyone who'd inspired any of my previous long walks – and many others were also inspired by books – actually join me on any of them. Even without the views Peel Fell felt like an appropriate place to start – the name probably means Boundary Mountain.

From Peel Fell the Watershed follows the rolling hills westwards. I would walk nearly 150 km before I turned north. Along the way I learnt that the Watershed was mostly free of obstructions other than fallen trees. Plantation forests often came up to it from both sides but there was always a rough, usually boggy, strip left free of trees. Here in the Borders the Watershed is also usually marked by a fence or wall as it was the natural boundary between estates, parishes, counties and local authorities. This made navigation easy, as long as I remembered to check for the right way at junctions. Following the fence that went up the highest visible hill wasn't always the right way. I had to remember what the Watershed was – the highest continuous line not the highest hills.

Alone now, the walk really began as I left Peel Fell for a tough day in rain, mist and wind that somewhat dampened the euphoria of starting out, though only a little. The first day of a long walk is always exciting. Initially I was on rough terrain covered with tussocks of heather and wiry grass interspersed with boggy hollows and peat hags but, later in the day, I reached the welcome shelter of the first of many Border conifer plantations and easy walking on forest tracks. The mist was still with me, drifting through the trees. Fascinating names came and went – Hartshorn Pike, Wheelrigg Head, Note O' The Gate, Dog Knowe, Wigg Knowe, Fenna Hill, Sandy Edge – Scots language names that sounded unfamiliar after the Gaelic hill names of home. The Watershed went up and down steep slopes in direct lines, something I would become used to in the weeks ahead. One descent down an initial boggy ride ended in landslips and a huge tangle of blown-down trees that took time and energy to clamber through, sometimes crawling under massive spiky fallen tree trunks, sometimes scrambling over them. Finally, I camped after a ten-hour, 24-km day on a hill called Black Rig on nice, firm, flat, sheep-cropped grass in the shelter of another plantation. I'd seen no-one all day and not much in the way of wildlife. I crawled gratefully into my shelter and removed my sodden shoes and socks. My soft and puffy wrinkled feet looked like prunes. It had been a tough first day. In my journal I wrote: 'the worst start weather of any long walk I've done'.

After ten hours' sleep I felt refreshed and ready for another day's tough walking. Looking out at mist and rain, I reflected that I've never had problems sleeping in a tent or even under the stars. The weather stayed that way until late afternoon as I went up and down a series of mostly boggy hills, ten in all, with every little bump named something Law, Head, Edge, Tooth or, most common, Hill. I finally camped between two of the latter, Comb Hill and Wisp Hill, under a clear sky. Most of the day I still had no real idea what the landscape I was walking through actually looked like until on the sixth summit, Todhope Hill, the mist cleared and there was

17

sunshine and high white cumulus clouds. Suddenly I could see big rounded hills, steep-sided and green, and as the world expanded so did my spirits. I could finally see the Watershed stretching out behind and in front of me, rolling over big rounded hills and giving focus and meaning to my journey. This is what I was here for.

Before climbing Comb Hill on steep grassy slopes, I descended equally steep slopes to the first deep cut in the Watershed where the A7 Edinburgh–Carlisle road slices through the hills. This is an old route and there's an old coaching inn close to the Watershed here. The Mosspaul Inn is one of the few buildings on or even close to the Watershed outside of a few places in the Lowlands. As a coaching inn it dates back to the 1760s. Before that, it seems, there was a chapel here, named for St Paul.

The inn has changed in the few years since I last passed by, and now self-catering accommodation is available but nothing else. Making an inn pay in such a remote location must be difficult, even with a main road running past the door. When I arrived, having been warned that it had closed, I was pleased to find that new owners had recently taken over, and food and beer was available. Although only on my second day out I followed the long-distance walkers' adage of never passing an opportunity for food. I would grow tired enough of the dried meals I was carrying in the weeks to come. I wouldn't heat one up that evening though, not after Portobello mushroom with stilton sauce and lots of vegetables followed by sticky toffee pudding with ice cream all washed down by shandy (I still had a hill to climb!) and coffee. It would turn out to be one of the best meals of the whole walk. Over dinner I had an interesting talk with the new landlady, Alison, who'd done much walking herself. Reminiscing about the Grand Canyon and Everest Base Camp, which we'd both visited, took me far away from the Watershed. Leaving the inn, the world seemed different, subdued and green and grey when my head was full of bright rocks, sparkling snow peaks and harsh sunlight.

Much revived by food and conversation, I charged up and over Comb Hill to eventually camp under a clear sky. Dawn arrived with sunshine and no clouds. Setting off in shorts, sunscreen and sunhat I felt this was going to be a good day. And it was, at first. Easy walking over a series of grassy hills gave excellent views over the rolling Southern Uplands. Buzzards wheeled over Wisp Hill. A fine black grouse shot into the air and away into the distance on Pikethaw Hill. Ahead lay the spiky skyline of Craik Forest, a huge conifer plantation. The map suggested that once in the trees there might not be any more water for quite a distance so at the oddly named Ewes Doors I drank deeply from a tiny trickle and filled a water bottle. It was not enough.

A pleasant lunch at Corbie Shank on the edge of the trees then it was into the morass. For mile after forest mile the Watershed was a mass of boggy tussocks that made for awful lurching slow progress. No rhythm, no speed. For six hours I staggered between the trees, barely managing more than a mile an hour. The forest was not attractive. Much of it consisted of clear-cut patches littered with debris interspersed with angular blocks of young trees: ugly and industrial. I preferred the sections in the mature forest – the trees might be crammed in dark rows but at least they felt natural and unsullied. My mood was not good. The lack of water didn't help. I was soon hot, sweaty and thirsty. The afternoon was muggy and the air in the forest felt stuffy and damp. There were no birds other than one cuckoo calling in the distance. There were flowers – white cloudberry in the bogs, and the yellow stars of lesser celandine, the delicate white of wood sorrel, purple violets and bright yellow buttercups on the edges of clear-cuts and in the boggy open slash of the Watershed, woodland flowers surviving from days when there was a more natural forest here and the sun could reach the ground. Under the crammed together conifers the ground was just piles of brown needles. Nothing living grew there. I camped in the trees by the first trickle I found, a functional site. I still had 14 km of forest ahead.

The Southern Uplands have little natural forest left. Much of the area is a mix of bare sheep-cropped hills, heather moorland and blocks of dark plantations, mostly Sitka spruce. Having already twice walked the Southern Upland Way, which runs coast to coast through the region, I knew this. I didn't though, know just how tough walking on the Watershed would be. The Southern Upland Way is a footpath. The Watershed isn't. The difference in the forest was proving huge.

Mostly planted in the 1960s and 1970s, forests like Craik were intended purely as sources of timber, with no thought given to wildlife, scenic qualities, or the landscape in general. Monoculture is not conducive to biodiversity or beauty. Attitudes are changing now – the days when planting such forests for tax purposes are gone, and the Forestry Commission tries to take scenic and amenity values into account along with wildlife. It will be a slow process to turn these vast forests into woods that are at least semi-natural and have a more varied fauna and flora.

I was woken by my phone signalling a message. Deep in the forest this was a surprise, especially as I thought I'd turned it off! The text was from my friend Tony Hobbs to say he was arriving in Moffat in two days' time to join me for a few days. Incentive enough to get through the forest. Moffat was some 34 km away. Not far but at the previous day's rate of progress it would take a long time.

Sitting up, I brushed against my shelter and felt a shower of cold water on my neck. The inside of the tarp was dripping with moisture. The night had been calm and humid and, with no wind to move the damp air, moisture had condensed on the walls. However, I could hear a few birds singing. Looking up, there were patches of blue in the narrow slit of sky visible between the trees. A cuckoo called loudly.

Another day of two halves ensued. The morning was a continuation of the previous afternoon as I struggled slowly through the boggy forest, a chore only broken by a short stretch on a forest road that paralleled the Watershed at a point where clear-cuts and new plantings made following the precise line complex and difficult. It was the first time I'd left the exact line by more than a few feet, at least knowingly, but I hadn't set out to stick rigidly to it anyway. My only aim was to follow it, either on or close to it, from start to finish in a continuous line. On this occasion the penalty for wandering off the Watershed was an extra kilometre's walking when I went the wrong way when returning. It was the first time I'd done this. It wouldn't be the last.

There were just two points of interest in the forest. The first was a faded battered sign on the summit of Craik Cross Hill headed Craik Signal Station that said the mound in front of the sign was believed to be a signal station on the Roman road between the forts at Raeburnfoot at Eskdalemuir and Trimontium near Melrose. I wondered what the place was like when the legions came marching through. It would have been a forest but a very different one to today's.

The second feature was a delight, a relief from the somewhat oppressive forest and the battlefield destruction of the felling. Suddenly the trees opened and, instead of the shattered remnants of a clear-cut, I saw blue water rippling in a breeze under a blue sky. This was Moodlaw Loch. Reeds rimmed the water and there was a feeling of wilder nature. I sat for a while, watching the water and relishing the escape from the industrial forest. All too soon though, I felt I had to push on along my narrow corridor in the trees. At one point there was an old little-used thin path, with signs indicating a mountain bike trail which ran a few km before disappearing, but basically it was tussocks again. Bags of little saplings ready for planting lined yet another clear-cut. I was pleased to see that they were deciduous trees, part of the softening of the forest. In the distance though, I could see lines of new conifers. Much of the forest won't change.

Finally, after crossing the empty Eskdalemuir to Ettrick road and a final plunge through the trees, I came out onto open hills and it was glorious! Suddenly I felt free. A strong cold wind blasted away the feelings of stuffiness. At times I could barely walk into it, but I could see. The world was big again. In the distance were wind turbines, dark forests lay below on every side, ahead bigger hills undulated above the trees. Suddenly I was walking twice as fast, relishing the feel of firm turf underfoot. Distance just zoomed by. Bloodhope Head, Mitchell Hill, Ettrick Pen, Hopetoun Craig and Wind Hill came and went, gentle summits on this long and broad high ridge. At one point the forest came up to the Watershed again on one side. Here the wind had pushed over the trees along the forest edge, leaving a great wall of earth and tree roots much taller than me.

From Wind Hill I descended to Ettrick Head where the Southern Upland Way crosses the Watershed and a sign marks the meeting of the Scottish Borders and Dumfries and Galloway: the Watershed as an administrative boundary again. Here I left the latter to head down the SUW to Moffat, Tony and resupply. Below Ettrick Head the path traverses a narrow ravine. On my two SUW walks I'd never really seen this, crossing it once in mist and rain and once in darkness, but it had felt wild and spectacular. This time I saw that it really was impressive, a deep rocky gash in the otherwise unbroken green slopes.

Camp was below this ravine in the shelter of more trees. A high camp had tempted me, but the wind made it seem unwise. After an eleven-hour day, I was now only a few hours from Moffat, and I was there early the next day to restock with food, eat in several restaurants, and book a room in the Stag Hotel. Tony arrived, and we had a pleasant evening discussing the next stage of the walk.

Moffat is a pleasant old town in scenic surroundings. It's mostly unspoilt and has many interesting buildings, the solidity of which keeps it just on the right side of being twee or quaint. It came to prominence as a spa town in the 1800s and was also a key market for wool. A large statue of a ram, given to the town in 1875, dominates the marketplace and is much photographed. Today tourism is a major industry. It was an excellent place for the first stopover of the walk.

Town stops are a break from walking, but also a busy time. This is when supplies are replenished, clothing washed, and contacts with the outside world made. I had reports for *The Great Outdoors* magazine to write too and the next morning saw me using the Rumbling Tum café as a base for writing my first piece, utilising Tony's phone for a Wi-Fi connection to send it in as my phone didn't like Moffat and refused to connect to anything.

Communications technology has changed the world of long-distance walking more than anything else. Designs and materials may have changed but tents are still tents, waterproof jackets still waterproof and rucksacks still big bags. I could have done this walk with the same gear I'd used on my first walk from Land's End to John o'Groats thirty-five years earlier. Back then though, the Internet and mobile phones were the ideas of science fiction. I sent postcards to the outdoor shop where I worked, and they moved a pin up a map of my route. Now I could post pictures and stories from my walk on the Internet whenever I got a signal and even, as I had the previous evening, sometimes send messages from a wild camp. Some say this diminishes the feel of wild places. I don't find it so. I still knew that I was responsible for myself, that the hills and woods needed care and skill to travel through safely and enjoyably. Better communication is simply a bonus. Mostly my smartphone was in airplane mode and just functioned as a camera and a GPS unit when I was walking anyway.

Moffat is a pleasant town, and I enjoyed the cafés and the hotel. I didn't want to stay long though, it was too soon in the walk for a rest day, and barely twenty-four hours after I arrived I was heading out, back up the Southern Upland Way to Ettrick Head and the Watershed. As on other long-distance walks my rule was that I'd walk an unbroken route, returning to the same place if I left the route to resupply. From Ettrick Head the Watershed does a big loop round Moffat Water, which cuts deeply into the hills, heading first roughly north-east and then back south-west. From Moffat I could have walked north some 9 km on the Annandale Way to re-join the Watershed at the great bowl of the Devil's Beef Tub. That would have been to miss a long section of the Watershed – a wonderful one too – so instead Tony and I walked some 60 km along the hills either side of Moffatdale to the Devil's Beef Tub.

The first day out from Moffat we only went as far as Ettrick Head where we camped on the edge of the forest. A figure came up out of the trees on the Southern Upland Way, the first other walker I'd seen since leaving Kielder. These are lonely hills. That night a few midges whined round our heads, the first of the walk. There would be more.

Walking with a companion is very different from walking solo. Even when apart and silent, there is always an awareness of company. Alone, decisions can be made on impulse. I sometimes find myself stopping and sitting down without consciously deciding to do so. I may find a lovely irresistible campsite after a few hours, I may walk well into the night, but with no-one to consult, no-one else's needs, desires, or tiredness need to be taken into account. There is also, I find, much more importantly, a closer connection to the land and to nature when there's no-one else to respond to, and it's that connection that lies at the heart of long-distance walking for me. So, my long-distance walks have been mainly solo, with friends joining for a few days here and there. Tony made for an amiable companion, as I knew from previous trips. We got on fine and he was happy to accord with my plans, so the walk continued as I wished. He was also blessed with the best continuous good weather of the walk so far with clear skies and sunshine and superb clarity.

The walk along the green rolling hills above Moffat Water was the highlight of the walk so far. The terrain made progress easy, the sun blazed down, and the views were tremendous, especially across Moffatdale to the bigger hills on the far side, deeply bitten into by steep-sided valleys. In one of these we could see a flush of brighter green spreading out from the valley floor and gradually fading as it reached the top of the slopes. This was the Carrifran Wildwood, where, since the year 2000, the Borders Forest Trust has planted over half a million native trees and shrubs with a view to restoring a semi-natural forest. This is a marvellous and heartening venture. Would that it could be replicated across the Southern Uplands.

Then came a dramatic view of the Grey Mare's Tail waterfall crashing down some 100 metres from the high valley holding Loch Skeen. In *The Waterfalls of Scotland*, Louis Stott says it's 'the most striking example of a hanging valley waterfall in the South of Scotland'. The Grey Mare's Tail and surrounding area is cared for by the National Trust for Scotland. Being so spectacular and easily accessible from a main road, it's very popular. It's also one of at least seven Grey Mare's Tail waterfalls in Scotland.

Seeing the waterfall was a sign that soon the Watershed would turn north-west and drop steeply to the head of Moffatdale and the A708 Moffat to Selkirk road, the second major road to cross the Watershed. There's a small cottage here, Birkhill, where the geologist Charles Lapworth stayed in the 1870s while he did pioneering work on the geology of the area.

The Southern Uplands were formed when what would become Scotland and England slowly converged as the ancient Iapetus Ocean closed, some 400 million years ago. The ocean floor was squeezed and buckled into the layers of greywacke sandstone and shale that form most of the region. The former rock doesn't have fossils; the latter does. Lapworth used the differences between the fossils in the different bands of shale to date the layers of rock.

The Watershed climbs from Birkhill, over a little hill called Watch Knowe, to run just east of Loch Skeen with a good view over this long hill loch and the crags that round its head, a touch of ruggedness rarely found in the Southern Uplands. A drystone wall and a fence mark the Watershed here and we camped by these on a calm, clear night.

Another split day followed, starting with glorious weather and the best walking so far as the Watershed swooped and soared over the big bold hills above Moffatdale. The sense of space and freedom, of striding out above the world, was exhilarating. This is what hillwalking is all about. From Firthhope Rig and Raven Craig we looked down into the greening Carrifran valley. Then it was up Hart Fell, at 808 metres the highest peak so far and the highest I would climb in the Southern Uplands. On went the fine walking, slowly descending over Barry Grain Rig and Chalk Rig Edge and Great Hill to Annandale Head where a fine big cairn marks the start of the excellent Annandale Way, a long-distance path that follows the River Annan from its source, here, to the Solway Firth. Below lies the deep hollow of the Devil's Beef Tub where Border Reivers are said to have hidden stolen cattle. Despite the fine weather there were no other walkers. Just those birds of the high moors, golden plovers and curlews piping and whistling, wild sounds in a wild place.

The Devil's Beef Tub is part of Corehead Farm, whose white buildings can be seen far below. This was bought by the Borders Forest Trust in 2009 and it's working towards restoring native woodlands, wetlands and heathlands alongside a farm operating on organic principles. Over 230,000 trees have already been planted, plus montane scrub species like downy willow high in the hills. Another part of the Southern Uplands is returning to nature.

Heading west we could see many wind turbines ahead, that gradually grew larger and came to dominate the view. This is the edge of the huge Clyde Wind Farm which covers 47.5 square km and has 152 turbines that run right up to the Watershed. It's built in another massive conifer plantation with areas cleared for the turbines and tracks.

Beyond Annanhead Hill the Watershed starts to turn north, away from the Moffat area, and soon descends to the A701 Dumfries to Edinburgh road. Once across this we entered the forest and reached the first wind turbines. For several km a wind farm track paralleled the Watershed some 50 to 100 feet away. As the going would otherwise be on rough boggy tussocks we followed it. A road sign read 'Array A 17km', giving us an inkling of the size of the wind farm.

Wind farms are a contentious issue in the Scottish hills as many have been built in places where they destroy any sense of peace or wildness, dominating the landscape even from afar. The Southern Uplands has been particularly affected. Conifer plantations are not wild or natural but they could be – simple neglect would see them return to a more natural state. Concrete wind turbines and tarmac roads will always be an intrusion. I'm not against all wind farms and I'm in favour of alternative green energy, but the location should always be taken into account and there should be a presumption against building them in wild areas. Peter Wright called the Watershed a ribbon of wildness because of its fairly unspoilt character with the potential to be a protected strip of nature running the length of the country. Having a giant wind farm almost touching it takes away greatly from this.

Not wanting to camp within sight or sound of the turbines we didn't think about stopping until we were well past them and could drop down to a little burn to pitch our tarps. We were now into the last section of the Watershed in the Southern Uplands. The next day we'd be in the Central Lowlands: aka Midland Valley. The last hills of the Southern Uplands made for a final walk on green rolling moors with rolling names. Risingclaw Heights, Wills Cleuch Head, Whitecamp Brae, North Black Dod, Cutter Cleuch Shank, Coomb Dod, Hillshaw Head, Gathersnow Hill, Glenwhappen Rig, Moss Law, Culter Fell, Kings Bank Head, Scawdmans Hill, Gawky Hill. For the final time every little top was named, wonderful names that rolled off the tongue. I wouldn't remember what each one was like, just a series of undulating rounded summits, but the names would bring back the walking over them. Looking at the map I could see that the Watershed here separated two of Scotland's major rivers, the Clyde and the Tweed, one noted for the heavy industry of shipbuilding in Glasgow, the other for salmon fishing and quiet countryside.

Ahead, we could soon see the flatlands. Soft terrain with neat fields, strips of woodland, roads, villages and towns. It didn't look like backpacking country. The Southern Uplands end abruptly, the hills falling to the valley floor. The underlying geology shifted and with it the landscape. The walk was changing. A steep descent from Gawky Hill and we crossed the Southern Upland fault, where the hills gave way to rich green fields, farms and country lanes lined with leafy trees. At one point the Watershed was both narrow and low, only a few km in width and a few metres in height separating the River Clyde and Biggar Water, which runs into the Tweed. There was no sense of this on the ground though. In the hills the Watershed rolling out ahead had usually been clearly visible, its line easily picked out. Down here that distinctiveness was lost. Only the map showed that this was the Watershed.

The first town soon appeared. Biggar lies close to the Watershed and was my next supply point. It was also where Tony would depart, catching a bus back to Moffat after four days. I would walk with no-one else for the rest of the walk. Setting off from Peel Fell I'd known that Tony would soon be joining me, but now I really was on my own. I'd been out for nine days and had walked 188 km, but the walk felt like it was just beginning

In Biggar we celebrated with a meal, beer and a night indoors at the Elphinstone Hotel. Two nights in my case. I hadn't had a complete day off yet and I knew from previous long walks that after nine to ten days a rest day – a zero day (i.e. no miles) in American long-distance hiking parlance – was wise or I'd start to slow down and feel tired. I wasn't racing or trying to break records. I wanted to appreciate the journey. The point of a long walk for me is to immerse myself in nature, to feel absorbed into the landscape.

Biggar wasn't so big as to feel overwhelming, which can be the case when you come down from the hills to a town or city. I could see countryside and hills beyond its confines. It's a pleasant market town (a royal burgh since 1451) with many fine old buildings and small enough to have avoided most of the generic shops and signage that give too many towns a bland identikit look.

In many respects it reminded me of Grantown-on-Spey, my local town for nigh on thirty years, and was big enough to offer all the amenities I needed. The rest day was actually a chores day, as they always are. It just didn't involve much walking. Maps were sent home, new ones collected from the Post Office. Clothes were washed. Emails and texts sent. Social media and blog posts made. A little food was purchased. In the next week I expected a plethora of places to eat so there seemed no need to carry much.

The first days of any long walk are a breaking-in period, a time for getting used to the rhythms of walking and camping, a time for sorting out any teething problems with gear and body, a time for shaking off the world left behind, a time for dealing with any initial worries and concerns. I'd done all that now. The walk really had begun, not just physically but mentally.

Ahead I had the section of the walk I was least looking forward to: crossing the Lowlands. I'd walked across the area once before, on my Land's End to John o'Groats walk. The Central Lowlands are only 80 km wide and I'd taken the shortest possible route straight across the edge of Glasgow to the sanctuary of the Campsie Fells and then the Highlands. It took me three days. The Watershed, however, took a meandering line for some 175 km and would take me over a week. Peter Wright praised the area in his book, but I suspected he was talking it up. I thought I knew what it was like and that I really wouldn't enjoy walking through it. I was so sure of this that I was tempted to cut this section short and avoid what I was convinced would be a rather tedious walk through fields, along farm tracks and minor roads, through villages and towns, and always in sight of busy roads and industry with little feel of the wild and few, if any, opportunities for wild camping. I was completely wrong.

3

THE SURPRISING CENTRAL LOWLANDS

Whilst I had thought of the Central Lowlands as a large flat area of farmland, industry, roads and towns between much more interesting hill country, it proved to be quite complex and diverse with plenty of hills of its own. In geological terms it's a graben or rift valley, a sunken block of the earth between the parallel lines of the Highland Boundary and Southern Upland Faults. The geology is complicated with many different rock types and structures, but the key elements are the Carboniferous strata holding the coalfields that fuelled Scotland's industrial heartland. In the Carboniferous period, around 300 million years ago, the land that would become Scotland was tropical, and organic sediments that were laid down in seas and swamps became coal. There was volcanic activity too, and there are many volcanic remnants in the Central Lowlands, the most notable being rugged Arthur's Seat in Edinburgh. I would see signs of these volcanoes in the Campsie Fells at the end of my Central Lowlands walk.

The first few hours out of Biggar appeared to confirm my ideas of what walking through the Central Lowlands would be like as I negotiated fences, followed the edges of ploughed fields, and wandered down farm tracks. Cows grazed in lush buttercup meadows. There were a few pretty corners, but the land felt tame. A sign carved on a gate entertained me briefly:

> *Be Ye Man Or Wumman*
> *Be Ye Suin Or Late*
> *Be Ye Gaein Or Comin*
> *Be Shair Taie Shut This Gate.*

I did, of course. Under the sign was another, faded, one. *Beware of the Bull*. If there was one I never saw him.

Ahead I could see a conical hill and after a few hours I was following the fence line that marked the Watershed to the top of 516-metre Black Mount where my world changed back to heather and grass moorland. From the crumbling trig point on the summit I could see more hills not far ahead: the south-eastern edge of the Pentland Hills, which I would soon reach. The slopes of Black Mount and its lower neighbour White Hill were steep too. Now I was definitely hillwalking.

A short stretch of farmland and lanes and I was climbing gradually into the Pentland Hills. This end of the range is gentler and less distinctive than the more popular northern part, close to Edinburgh. There were rough tracks and patches of burnt moorland, indicating grouse shooting country. Much of the land was covered with heather, coarse grass and reeds with, on North Muir, some of the most extensive areas of cotton grass I've ever encountered. I camped on the drier northern slopes of this hill. There was no sight or sound of people. I could see and hear curlews, lapwings, oystercatchers, skylarks, cuckoos and crows. A kestrel hovered. A buzzard flew low over the moorland. It felt as wild and remote as any camp so far. There was a surprising sense of space. I hadn't expected this.

Listening to the birds I recalled that, in the farmland areas, I had heard and seen many songbirds in the hedgerows and little woods, and rooks and pigeons in the fields. There were flowers too: bluebells, pink campion and white stitchwort in the hedgerows, yellow tormentil on the hills. In the Southern Uplands I had seen little wildlife. I hadn't expected this either. I'd assumed that the wilder, remoter areas would have the most birds and animals. Thinking about it though, I realised that, visually attractive though the great sweeping green hills of the Southern Uplands are, they are ecologically impoverished, as are the, less pleasing to the eye, conifer plantations. Projects like Carrifran and Corehead are changing this but most of the area is sadly not much suited to wildlife. Down here there was a greater diversity of habitat that could support much more. I would think about this a great deal over the next few days.

Setting up camp is for me one of the pleasures of long-distance walking. I love creating a temporary home in the wilds. By now I had established a routine that meant I could have camp established very quickly. Once I'd found a suitable site – dry, flat, sheltered from the wind if necessary and ideally with a good view – I set down my pack and took out my shelter. I wasn't using a tent but rather a tarp – a shaped sheet of waterproof nylon that I could pitch with my walking poles and which was, in fact, more storm resistant than most lightweight tents whilst also being much roomier. The Trailstar was to prove a star of the walk.

Using a tarp rather than a tent does surprise and even shock some people. I once used it when I was asked to do a short piece on winter camping in the Cairngorms for a BBC TV *Countryfile Winter Special* and was filmed pitching it and climbing into my sleeping bag before being left with an infrared camera to do some night filming after the crew had returned to their hotel. They came back early in the morning to film me having breakfast. When the clip was shown one viewer berated the programme for 'making that poor man sleep under a sheet!' Actually, I'd been quite comfortable. As it was winter I'd used only a groundsheet inside the Trailstar. On this walk, because of the likelihood of midges, I had a mesh inner to hang inside.

With the Trailstar erected I set up my kitchen in the doorway: a methylated spirits burner that sat inside a clever cone that doubled as windshield and pot support. It was very light, simple to use and had no roaring flame to block the sounds of nature. I had two titanium pots. One for eating from and a smaller one for a mug. Both could be used to boil water. Inside the Trailstar I laid my insulating mat over the hard, bumpy and cold ground and then my sleeping bag, shaking it to fluff up the goose down filling. If chilly I'd slide half into the bag and cook and eat from there.

Otherwise I sat in the doorway watching the darkening sky. To hand I'd have my notebook and pen for writing up my thoughts on the day and my Kindle e-reader, which held a library of books including *Ribbon of Wildness* – I view e-readers as one of the greatest developments for long-distance walking in recent years. I used to carry a paperback or two. Now I could carry a library for the weight of one of them. During this part of the walk I was reading Wade Davis's excellent and long *Into the Silence: the Great War, Mallory and the Conquest of Everest*. I would never have carried the weighty printed book. I also had outdoor-themed books by Jim Crumley, Alex Roddie, Jim Perrin, Graham Forbes, Robert Macfarlane, George Monbiot, Kellan MacInnes, Andy Kirkpatrick, Keith Foskett, and Nan Shepherd. I would never get bored during rainy evenings in camp.

When camp was complete I was all set for a pleasant evening. If it rained I'd retreat further into the Trailstar; if dry I'd fall asleep with my head in the doorway, so I'd wake to the outdoors rather than surrounded by nylon. I find camping like this simple and delightful. On this occasion I watched the sun's orange glow fading in the west and the clouds overhead turning black and fading into the night. Come the dawn, I sat outside as the sun warmed the land, watching the moors return to life and listening to the birds. It was a relaxing start to the day and I lingered long over breakfast.

Having meandered north-eastwards from Biggar, the Watershed was now at its easternmost point in the Central Lowlands. From North Muir it turned back northwards and, for several hours, I crossed the lonely heather moors of the southern Pentland Hills. I saw no-one, just waders, sheep and the occasional grouse. In the boggy areas as well as cotton grass I found the lovely white flowers of cloudberry. There were some rough paths and tracks and Scottish Rights of Way and Access Society signposts but nothing to indicate anybody had been here for quite a while. On the highest summit in the area, 518-metre Craigengar, the waters running off the Watershed to my right finally ceased to end up in the River Tweed. Now they ended up in the Forth.

Craigengar marks the closest the Watershed comes to Edinburgh, Scotland's capital and a city I had come to know and love over the years, though there was a very long gap between my first visit and my second. In my last year at St Peter's Church of England Primary School in Formby, on the Lancashire coast, I came on a school trip to Scotland, the first time I'd visited the country. We split our time between Edinburgh and Glasgow. I have only a few memories of the trip now. I was keen on castles at the time so visits to those in Edinburgh and Stirling have stayed with me. My main memory though, is discovering hillwalking and mountains, not something you'd expect from a stay in a city. However, Edinburgh has the rugged volcanic Arthur's Seat.

Although only 251 metres high, Arthur's Seat has the characteristics of a mountain. It's rocky, steep, and there are crags. I'd never seen anything like it – in Formby 10-metre sand dunes were the highest hills for miles. I was fascinated by the sight of it rising above the houses and felt a strong desire to climb it. It wasn't on the itinerary though and the teachers were not interested. So, I roped in another boy and went anyway, finding our way through the streets and then clambering up to the summit. I remember feeling elated and excited. Finding our way back was rather more difficult but we did manage; as far as I remember we only got a mild telling-off for disappearing for many hours. I don't think teachers would be so unbothered at two eleven-year-olds wandering off into Edinburgh these days.

Though I didn't realise it for many, many years, that ascent of Arthur's Seat was very significant, giving me a love of mountains, wild land, hillwalking and exploration. It was to be over forty years before I climbed it again. When I first lived in the Highlands I didn't visit Edinburgh except to change trains, having no interest in cities. Two factors changed this. One was my step-daughter going to Edinburgh College of Art, the other was discovering the Edinburgh Festivals. Hazel now lives close to the Pentlands and I thought of her as I crossed them. I could have been at her home in a day.

It was my partner who persuaded me to attend the Festivals, something she'd done a few times many years before. To my surprise I found that as well as the plays and concerts I enjoyed the excitement of the crowded streets, the entertainers, colour, liveliness and the whole feeling of being part of an arts explosion. That said, after a week or so I start thinking about the hills and the first day I usually wander around in a daze. We've been many times now and it was on one of these trips that I climbed Arthur's Seat again. I now try to do so each summer.

Having shaken off my prejudice against cities I found Edinburgh fascinating. I love the contrast between the straight lines and neat formality of the New Town and the warren-like tangle of the Old Town where I'm still discovering sets of steps and narrow alleys. Arthur's Seat, the Castle on its crag, and Calton Hill with its collection of monuments give the city a distinctive look. The wonderful National Museum of Scotland is always visited and there are usually exhibitions at the art galleries or the National Library that attract me too.

Sometimes just wandering the streets and admiring the many varied buildings can occupy half a day. I love some of the modern buildings as well as the old ones, including the oft criticised Scottish Parliament Building which I think is magnificent inside and out, a modern home for our new parliament (the disdain for it as a building, I suspect, is often a dislike of the whole idea of a Scottish Parliament). I love the inscriptions from Scottish writers on the Canongate Wall of the parliament and always look at these. Unsurprisingly my favourites are these:

'The battle for conservation will go on endlessly. It is part of the universal battle between right and wrong.'

John Muir

'What would the world be, once bereft
Of Wet and Wildness, let them be left,
O let them be left, wildness and wet;
Long live the weeds and the wilderness yet.'

Gerard Manley Hopkins. *Inversnaid*

I hope the Parliamentarians inside always remember these words.

I also always visit the Makars' Court at The Writers' Museum where the words of more writers are inscribed in the paving stones. Here I seek out the words of Nan Shepherd, author of *The Living Mountain*, one of the finest books on mountains and the mountain experience ever written. The quotation here isn't from that book but from her novel *The Quarry Wood*.

'It's a grand thing, to get leave to live.' Nan Shepherd.

The Scottish Parliament didn't exist when I moved to Scotland and wouldn't do for another ten years. The debate about whether there should be a Scottish Parliament and what powers it should have, which took place in the run-up to the 1997 referendum on the issue was the first time I felt engaged in specifically Scottish politics. Although my interest in conservation matters was becoming more and more Scotland-centred I hadn't connected it with Scottish politics, mainly because the latter didn't really seem to exist, everything being decided in Westminster. The idea of a Scottish Parliament appealed to me – I had always thought having power as close to people as possible was a good thing and that a network of small democratic countries and regions co-operating was far better than big centralised ones run from the top down. It's an old adage, but I think 'power corrupts' is usually true so a system where no-one has that much power nor has it for a long time is probably the best we can come up with.

I was looking forward to the referendum and ready to vote for a parliament. However, I was unable to do so as I was in hospital having my appendix removed after being taken ill while out researching a book on walks in the Ben Nevis and Glencoe areas. I was most annoyed, but relieved when the vote was massively in favour of the parliament. If it had been lost by one vote I'd have felt guilty!

So, 300 years since the last Scottish Parliament had been abolished by the Treaty of Union with England, Scotland had its own parliament again. I remember feeling pleased but unsure whether it would have a direct effect on my life. It would and quickly. One of the first pieces of legislation passed was the National Parks Act which led to the creation of Scotland's first two national parks, Loch Lomond and the Trossachs, and the Cairngorms, in the next few years. That Scotland, the birthplace of the great conservationist John Muir who was known in the USA as the father of national parks, didn't already have national parks was a disgrace. Ten years earlier I wouldn't have known why but now I understood this was because of rule from London. Ten national parks were created in England and Wales in the 1950s; none in Scotland. There wasn't enough desire south of the border and the landowning interests in the House of Lords (having an unelected chamber is another disgrace) who didn't want national parks ensured they didn't happen.

As I was living in Grantown-on-Spey in the Cairngorms I became involved in the plans for the Cairngorms National Park. I'd been persuaded to represent the Mountaineering Council of Scotland (now Mountaineering Scotland) on the Cairngorms Recreation Forum, one of many such forums set up by the non-statutory Cairngorms Partnership, which met in Grantown in what are now the national park offices. We spent much time poring over plans from government agency Scottish Natural Heritage for the areas the park might cover. The final result was closer to the Forum's view than some of the proposals. I was happy with it. It included my home! I'd always wanted to live in a national park (the Lake District was my first choice when I was in England) but had never thought I would be able to afford it. Now I knew the secret. Move first and then have the park created around you.

Scotland's national parks have had teething troubles and certain actions and decisions have led to some erstwhile supporters becoming disillusioned. I'm still on the optimistic side and think that the positives outweigh the negatives. Just letting them get on with it is not wise though (it never is), and I do think those concerned with nature, wild land, and access should criticise the parks and call for change when they get it wrong. And, of course, praise them when they do good things. It's never black and white. I'd also like to see more national parks, many more. On this walk I'd traverse Loch Lomond and the Trossachs National Park from south to north but would only brush the edge of the Cairngorms.

A second piece of legislation would have a much more direct effect on me. In 2003 the parliament passed the Land Reform Act which included a right of access for non-motorised travel and for wild camping on virtually all land. This was breakthrough legislation and, again, something that would never have happened without a Scottish Parliament. I was only slightly involved in the campaign and am extremely grateful to those who led it. They included the late billionaire owner of the Letterewe estate in the NW Highlands, Paul van Vlissingen, who in the 1990s agreed the Letterewe Accord on access rights, which became the basis of the Scottish Outdoor Access Code in the access legislation, Dave Morris of Ramblers Scotland, Bob Reid of the Mountaineering Council of Scotland, and the late Alan Blackshaw who produced definitive statements on the legal position before the Act (and who was the author of one of the first outdoor instruction manuals I ever bought, an influential and comprehensive book called simply *Mountaineering*).

Many more played a key part – John Mackenzie the Earl of Cromartie (who later persuaded me to succeed him as the President of the then Mountaineering Council of Scotland, which was not a good idea as I wasn't suited to the task of effectively being chair of a board of directors – I remember the time I was told of my duties as line manager – I had no idea what a line manager was), and Cameron McNeish, a friend for many years, who was great at taking the arguments to the public.

Ironically, a very unpleasant event also had a major influence on the access legislation. This was the foot and mouth outbreak of 2001 when the countryside was shut for many weeks for fear people would spread the disease. Just before the outbreak began, parliament had published draft access legislation that, in many ways, would have made the situation worse as trespass would become a criminal as opposed to a civil offence, and access rights would only apply during daylight hours. With those barely being six hours in the Highlands in winter such a restriction would have penalised day-walkers as well as making wild camping illegal all year round. Landowners behaving badly changed all that. Some of them used foot and mouth as an excuse to keep land closed unjustifiably (there were 'Keep Out' signs in some locations for many months after it ended). The reaction from the politicians was to change the legislation and put their trust in those taking access rather than the owners of the land.

The access legislation has worked pretty well, though it can't be taken for granted and does need policing (at the time of writing it's depressing that one of the worst offenders against the spirit of the legislation is Loch Lomond and the Trossachs National Park).

Does the access legislation really make a difference? It does, psychologically as well as in practice. Just knowing that there is a right to walk and camp on land is significant. I've absorbed that now and am shocked when I go elsewhere and discover I don't have those rights. On this walk it made a difference to where I walked and camped, especially in this Lowlands section where I was closer to farms, towns and roads. On previous long walks in Scotland I'd always been careful to hide away when camping anywhere near roads or buildings. I'd only once been asked to move but that was because I was usually where no-one was likely to see me.

For short trips in the deer stalking season I'd stuck to places where there wasn't blanket access restrictions. My continuous round of all the Munros and Tops, seven years before the access legislation, had run into the stalking season. I'd continued but had been very careful to avoid any stalking parties. On one occasion on spotting off-road vehicles and men with guns heading up the Strathfarrar Munros I'd walked down the glen and climbed them from the other direction, taking my time so I'd be descending long after they'd gone. Under the access legislation estates can't have blanket bans covering whole hill areas and lasting for weeks or months. Requests to stay away are allowed for specific days and specific areas (a named corrie, for example). This is reasonable, and I've been happy to accord with it.

Where the legislation has made the biggest difference is in lowland areas, especially around towns and cities where opportunities for access were often restricted, there being few legal rights of way, a designation that doesn't matter now. Since the Act was passed new paths have sprung up in many areas, in part because it became obvious that people now expected them, and because some landowners realise that people prefer to use paths and will stick to them when provided.

All in all, the Scottish Parliament has proved valuable for outdoors people. The debate now is over wild land and conservation. Not everything the parliament does in this regard is desirable, but I think the situation would be far worse if all the decisions were being made in Westminster. I feel it's much easier to have a say in Scotland and to influence the parliament and therefore more worth trying than I ever felt about Westminster. I've come to think of the Scottish Parliament as *our* parliament and the Scottish Government as *our* government. Westminster has always been the government, the parliament.

I thought about all this as I crossed the Pentlands, knowing the parliament wasn't far away.

I wasn't visiting Edinburgh on this walk, close though it was. Cities don't usually lie on or near watersheds. They arise on coasts and by big rivers, water providing the quickest and easiest way to travel and to transport goods until the railways and then motor vehicles arrived. Scotland's two biggest cities, Glasgow and Edinburgh, are fairly close to the Watershed because the country is at its narrowest here, with just 40 km separating the Firth of Clyde from the Firth of Forth. In a few days I'd be looking across to tower blocks on the edge of Glasgow. Edinburgh I never saw at all.

As I slowly descended from the Pentlands to the A70, more and more wind turbines appeared ahead. These would dominate the remainder of the day as I passed Muirhall and then the much bigger Black Law wind farms (the latter is the biggest in the UK). This is a former mining and quarrying area with much industrial detritus that is now used mainly for farming and commercial forestry. I'm very much in favour of renewable energy but not at the expense of our wild places. This is where wind farms should be sited. Sheep grazed in fields below the spinning turbines. A buttercup meadow shone in the late afternoon sunshine, the bright yellow flowers and vivid green grass giving beauty to the landscape.

In search of a meal I diverted a few km to the old mining village of Forth. The first industry here was weaving, but this was replaced by ironstone and limestone quarrying and coal mining as the industrial revolution took hold. The mines closed in the 1960s and 1970s as heavy industry declined. The railway station had gone in 1955. Much of the old mining area has been returned to moorlands and wetlands, dotted with large conifer plantations. And now there's a new energy source replacing coal: wind power. That doesn't employ the numbers mining did though, and neither does forestry.

I found the town nondescript and a little run-down. This was not Moffat and Biggar. However, the people were friendly, and it had the amenities I wanted. As I wandered down the main street two men smoking outside a bar greeted me, a walker with a big pack being an unusual sight. Nobody had noticed in Moffat and Biggar. I told them about the walk. They showed interest and surprise, having never heard of the Watershed. I suspect they thought I was a bit crazy but harmless and providing a little distraction. They recommended a restaurant, The Inns, and it did provide a tasty and filling meal.

If there'd been a B&B or hotel in Forth I might have stayed, but this wasn't a place people come to visit so there was no accommodation. I headed back to the Watershed which soon entered a spruce plantation. Whilst the blocks of conifers weren't very attractive, they did offer shelter for a secluded camp in this rather open landscape. In an area of low rolling moorland called the Gladsmuir Hills I pitched my tarp on a long disused overgrown old forest track. Birds were singing but I could also hear traffic on nearby roads. Midges kept me inside my shelter.

I was woken by a wonderful dawn chorus at 4 a.m. I hadn't heard anything approaching this number of birds before. The variety of habitats here, although small, was clearly valuable for bird life. More so, it seemed, than much of the Southern Uplands. As the day got under way the birds were joined by some mechanical clanging from not far away. Visually my campsite wasn't unattractive. Looking out of the doorway I could see long grass, a fallen tree trunk, and to either side rows of Sitka spruce. As with other plantations it felt better inside than it looked from outside.

After the walk I checked my 1978 Land's End to John o'Groats journal and found that I'd camped in the Gladsmuir Hills then, in what I described as 'new forestry plantations'. I guess they were, but that was thirty-five years ago. I'd walked here in a day from Biggar, where I'd also resupplied, passing through Forth, which I described as dreary and set in a sad rural-industrial wasteland of old abandoned mines, bare spoil heaps, ragged smallholdings and deserted buildings. There had certainly been improvements since then. The landscape now was a curious mix of semi-wild land, gradually greening industrial decay, shadowed dark conifer woods, and rich farmland with the shining spinning white wind turbines adding a strange sci-fi post-apocalyptic look. It wasn't urban, rural, or wild but something else, something with a future that looks towards the last two, which is good.

'June 10 became ill!' My journal entry for the day that followed the Gladsmuir Hills camp, for once written several days later, was blunt and to the point. The worst two days of the walk were beginning, the only days I really didn't enjoy much.

Not long after setting off I diverted into Shotts, another somewhat run-down but friendly old coal mining town. Here I bought some food, including a cheese and onion sandwich. I was to be very suspicious of that sandwich later.

Back on the Watershed I crossed the low semi-wild Cant Hills, which did give some extensive views of the industrial and farming lands all around. In the distance I could hear a constant low rumbling that gradually grew louder and louder. The sound of traffic on the busy M8 motorway. Soon I could see the vehicles zooming along, roaring through the landscape, a jolting sight as I was now attuned to the speed of walking and hadn't seen that many vehicles since setting off. Certainly, nowhere near this many or going so fast. On the far side of the racing traffic lay a large working quarry taking a big bite out of the hillside and out of the Watershed. Somehow it seemed appropriate to have this rising above the streaking metal boxes and the hard curves of the road.

Before crossing the M8 I reached the Kirk O'Shotts, often known as the M8 Church. This dates from 1821 but there was a church here for hundreds of years before that. Nearby is St Catherine's or Kate's Well where water gushes out of a stone spout. An inscribed boulder gives the date of the well as AD 1411. I filled my water bottles here. In wild places away from buildings, roads and livestock I drink from streams and pools without treating the water. The pleasure of drinking fresh cold water is one I am loath to abandon. On this walk I was carrying some water purification tablets in case I had to drink suspect water. I never used them. On this Lowlands section I was more cautious when in farmland and industrial areas and mostly got water in towns. Kate's Well being a natural spring I reckoned the water would be fine. Maybe I was wrong, or maybe it was that sandwich.

Luckily, there's a footbridge over the M8 close to the Watershed. Soon, the traffic noise was fading and I crossed Duntilland Hill before climbing to an array of huge transmission masts on Black Hill. Here I ate the sandwich. And drank some of the water. Shortly afterwards I felt very bloated and a little unwell. This was only the start.

Difficult boggy walking led through the Torrance conifer plantation to the edge of huge Cairneyhill Quarry. Peering down I could see tiny dumper trucks buzzing round the quarry floor. The edge was fenced and 'Danger Keep Out' signs warned of high faces and loose rock. This was the most industrial and least natural spot on the Watershed yet. Or so it seemed. But, right on the rim of the quarry I came on a delightful little loch set in gentle moorland. There were birds on the water and, feeling tired and not quite right, I lay in the heather for a while and watched them. Canada geese and a large flock of mallard ducks sailed quietly by. Much noisier were some moorhens that clacked mechanically as they bobbed up and down. I saw other wildlife during the day too – a badger nosing about in a field, roe deer and grey squirrels in the forests. The Central Lowlands may not be 'wild' but there's plenty of wildlife.

Feeling more and more ill I didn't try to follow the intricate line of the Watershed through farmland, moorland and dere-lict industrial wasteland for the next few miles, but instead took tracks and roads close to it. This didn't look like walk-ing or wild camping country. In fact, it was the most damaged land along the whole Watershed. There were hills: strangely smooth conical ones, some bare, some grassed over. These were bings, huge piles of the spoil from coal mines. One particularly notable one, known as the Mexican Hat, is now part of a scheduled monument, the remains of Lochend Colliery Pit No.5, which was worked from about 1880 to 1948 and is one of the best preserved. How quickly the thriving working industry of one era can become the historic monu-ments of the next, places to visit and study to find out how a previous generation lived and worked. The dirt, the noise, the miners are all gone. Just quiet now. A spoil heap becoming a hill, empty buildings fading away.

Not that I thought this at the time. Given how I was feeling I just wanted to find somewhere indoors to curl up and not have to deal with camping. That, in itself, told me I was ill.

Soon I reached the only large town on the Watershed, Cumbernauld, where I was glad, for once, to book into an anonymous identikit Premier Inn. I didn't want to speak much to anyone, it seemed too much effort. I had no appetite and ate nothing that evening. My stomach was churning. During the night and on and off the next day I vomited and had frequent diarrhoea. Something horrible was happening to my insides. The sandwich or the well water? Impossible to say but I regretted both.

Bad stomach upsets are always a ghastly experience. On a long walk they're even worse as you feel weak and exhausted as well as sick, and usually can't continue for a day or two. Long-distance walkers fear such illness and consequently some filter or purify all water. Research shows that this doesn't necessarily work; walkers still get sick. The evidence suggests this may be due to not washing hands regularly after going to the toilet and then sharing food and eating and drinking utensils. Just one person with unclean hands putting them into a bag of trail mix and then passing it round could spread a stomach bug. As I hadn't shared food with anyone that couldn't be the case on this occasion.

I'd never been ill like this on a long-distance walk before and I'd only ever treated water when it looked nasty and there was no alternative – muddy cattle ponds covered with green slime or tiny stagnant smelly puddles on which dead insects floated. Mostly I just drank the water straight and was fine. I was usually alone though and rarely sharing food with anyone else. I have had people tell me I must have a cast-iron stomach.

I don't, and if that implies being immune to all stomach bugs then nobody does.

I have had awful stomach upsets on walks before, three times in fact, all on treks in Nepal. On those trips I took great care with water, hygiene and food. I was leading organised groups with trek crews who boiled and treated all water, but still got sick. On one trip it was just me, on two it was others as well, but never the whole group. Food, water, something else? I didn't know. The experiences were vile though. I remember a sleepless night vomiting and almost delirious followed by an unreal stagger to Everest Base Camp, punctuated by dives off the trail at frequent intervals. Walking while this ill was probably a stupid thing to do but as the group leader I felt obliged to continue. On another occasion I only became ill as we were about to fly home, spending the flight curled up on the floor of a toilet cubicle.

In Cumbernauld, moving on the next day seemed unwise. I probably wouldn't have got far anyway as I felt so tired and weak. Knowing what walking was like when feeling like this, I was sensible enough not to try. So, it was a second night in the hotel. I hadn't intended to spend a day in Cumbernauld. In fact, I'd planned on walking straight through. I made one short venture into the tangle of roads, supermarkets and shopping malls that makes up the centre. Cumbernauld is a new town built in the 1950s. It has a population of 52,000 and was by far the biggest place I would pass through or divert to for supplies on the whole walk.

Cumbernauld is not actually a bad town for walkers as there is much green space and many footpaths, footbridges and underpasses. I did find negotiating these somewhat difficult though. Sometimes I could see where I wanted to go but not how to get there without risking dashing across busy roads. I wasn't used to towns! As well as some food for the next few days, which I bought whilst trying not to think about it, I needed a couple of tent pegs to replace some I'd lost and hoped to find a hat to replace my much-loved Tilley Hat, which I'd left, a week before, in the Stag Inn in Moffat (and which my partner had arranged to have sent home. I'd have been sad to lose it). A week ago! The thought stopped me. It seemed much longer than that. The big green hills of the Southern Uplands felt a world away, yet it was only four days earlier that I'd left them behind. I was fully immersed in the Lowlands now. Cumbernauld is not a place for outdoor gear and I could find only heavy steel tent pegs in packets of ten in the camping section of a supermarket. I left eight behind. For hats there were only baseball caps garnished with garish slogans that I really didn't want to wear. Finally, I found a dull grey cotton peaked cap in Asda. It cost just £5 and was to prove fine.

With my appetite slowly returning I bought and ate a spicy pizza for dinner on a kill or cure basis. It was kill and another night of illness followed. I felt like an idiot. By morning I was drained but also bored, a sign, I hoped, that I was recovering. The day before I'd been too ill for boredom to be an issue. Late in the morning, having eaten nothing and drunk only water, I thought my delicate stomach might cope with walking so I set off gingerly. A footbridge took me over the busy M80 motorway into lush green countryside with tree-lined paths and rich flower meadows. Looking back, Cumbernauld slowly faded into the trees. The only urban section of the Watershed was over.

Soon I reached a straight shallow depression running through the fields, under hawthorns in full creamy bloom and into woodland. This was the line of the Antonine Wall, for a short while the north-west frontier of the Roman Empire. It's less well known than Hadrian's Wall to the south, probably because it consisted of a turf bank and a ditch rather than a stone wall. It was built by Hadrian's successor, Antoninus Pius, who was Emperor from AD 138–161, around AD 142 but after only twenty or so years it was abandoned, and the frontier retreated to Hadrian's Wall. Running 37 km across the Central Lowlands from the Clyde to the Forth, it had seventeen forts plus smaller buildings that accommodated 6,000–7,000 legionaries. A military road south of the wall was used to move troops and supplies. From inscriptions we know that some of the soldiers came from faraway places like Syria, Algeria and Spain. I wondered what they made of the Scottish climate and if they were bothered by midges.

After the Romans left, the origins of the Antonine Wall were forgotten for almost a millennium and a half. Only in the eighteenth century was the story of the Grymisdyke, as it became known, rediscovered and with it interest in the wall. Today it's a UNESCO World Heritage Site and is managed by the Councils along its route in conjunction with Historic Scotland.

I reached the Antonine Wall near Tollpark where a notice said that the section of ditch in the wood was one of the best surviving sections. It was unbroken here, but I wouldn't have known what it was without the notice. It's not an obvious fortification like Hadrian's Wall.

Just north of the Antonine Wall is the main Glasgow–Edinburgh railway line and the Forth and Clyde Canal which I followed a short distance to Wyndford Lock. The canal was lined with trees and flower-rich banks and there were narrow boats on the water, making for an interesting and pleasant stroll. The vegetation was rich, the air heady with scents, the sky blue and the air warm. It felt like high summer. The tranquil surroundings were quite soothing and the walking easy, which I needed as my body felt quite battered, and I was walking slowly and carefully. Difficult terrain and stormy weather were not things I wanted to deal with. The Watershed is probably a kilometre to the west of Wyndford Lock according to Peter Wright, though he does point out that the construction of the canal and its associated embankments and drains makes the landscape hard to read here.

The 56-km canal was built between 1768 and 1790 and roughly parallels the Antonine Wall. Running from the River Clyde to the Firth of Forth it connects the Irish Sea with the North Sea. At a time when road travel was rough and slow it provided a fast way to move agricultural, mining and other produce and for fishing and other seagoing vessels to move from coast to coast without having to go the very long way round the north of Scotland. The canal was popular with passengers, and boats linked to coach services. At first the canal flourished but, as with other such waterways, competition from the railways and then motor vehicles led to decline. It was closed in 1963. However, after much restoration it was reopened in 2001 and the next year reconnected with the Union Canal via the Falkirk Wheel for the first time in over seventy years. The canal is now owned and managed by Scottish Canals.

From Wyndford Lock I climbed slowly through green fields to rougher moorland pasture dotted with clumps of windblown trees. Nodding fluffy, white flower heads of cotton grass appeared in boggier areas along with tussocks of rushes and reeds. Soon I reached a long line of low hills, a broad ridge known as the Kilsyth Hills that form the south-eastern outlier of the Campsie Fells. On the northern side the conifers of the Carron Valley Forest, a vast plantation running down to the Carron Valley Reservoir, ran up to the Watershed. To the south, open slopes ran down to flatlands. The

Watershed turns west here as it begins a long loop round the headwaters of the River Carron.

Following an old stone boundary wall that separated the trees from the open moor, I looked over the undulating expanse of the Central Lowlands, now fading into the distance. Tower blocks marked the Greater Glasgow conurbation, the largest built-up area in Scotland. From up here, even at an elevation of only 450 metres, it looked small and insignificant compared to the vastness of the world around. Towards the horizon the landscape was very hazy. I'd like to have seen Edinburgh and the Firth of Forth but try as I might I couldn't honestly say I did. I might have had better luck with the flash of light beyond Glasgow. Maybe it was the Firth of Clyde. It would have been nice to have seen both coasts from the Watershed here, where Scotland is at its narrowest, but it was not to be.

The sky was clear, the air calm and warm, and my guts weren't churning so, overall, I was content. I crossed the first named bump on the ridge, Tomtain, the hill of fire, and decided to camp as I was feeling tired after only 15 km. The after-effects of the illness would take some days to shake off. On the slopes of Garrel Hill I pitched my tarp on the tussocky ground, a pleasant site with widespread views. From the doorway I could see only hills, moorland grasses and trees and it felt quite wild and remote. A party of runners in vests and shorts trotted past, reminding me that towns and roads weren't far away.

The Campsie Fells, which I would cross in the next two days, are great slabs of layered lava flows from volcanic activity in the Carboniferous period, when the coalfields were also laid down. The name is now used for all the hills in this group though, originally, it applied only to the highest southern hills (according to Peter Drummond in his excellent book *Scottish*

Hill Names). He also points out that the use of 'fells' in the name is relatively modern, first appearing in print in 1790.

On Timothy Pont's late sixteenth-century map the name is 'The Muir of Campsie' and applies to the hills above the hamlet and church of Campsie. 'Fell', a name I'd encountered frequently in the Southern Uplands, is an Anglicisation of the Norse 'fjall', meaning mountain, and is found in areas occupied by the Vikings in northern England and southern Scotland and on some of the Hebrides in the form of the suffix – val, my favourite being Trollaval. You can't get much more Viking than that! Here in the Campsies, Drummond reckons the name didn't come directly from Norse but was a sign of the growing status of English amongst the Scots gentry and thus 'essentially artificial'. Drummond doesn't give a meaning for Campsie. Others suggest it may come from the Gaelic for crooked.

Being so close to Glasgow the Campsie Fells have played an important part in the story of the outdoors movement in Scotland. Generations of Glaswegians began their outdoor life here, exploring the hills they could see every day. Before many people had cars or the money to travel far, these were accessible hills. Two leading mountaineering writers and broadcasters who began their outdoor life with trips here from Glasgow are Tom Weir, who came here in the 1930s, and Cameron McNeish, whose first backpacking experience was some thirty years later. The Campsies were also the birthplace of Scottish skiing. In 1892, W. W. Naismith, he of the eponymous Naismith's Rule (for calculating times for hill ascents), skied here, the first person to try skiing in the Scottish hills.

On my first night in the Campsies I slept for twelve hours. The first day's walking after my illness had exhausted me. I woke myself up with a mug of the coffee powder I'd bought in a supermarket in Cumbernauld. It wasn't the caffeine that woke me though but the taste. It was disgusting! 'Just about drinkable with sugar. Mix with hot chocolate or decaf in future', I wrote in my journal. I didn't usually put sugar in coffee – I carried it to mix with muesli – and the decaffeinated coffee was for the evenings when I didn't want to be kept awake. That I was considering drinking it at breakfast shows just how awful the supermarket coffee was.

Streaks of high cloud sped across the sky and there was a cool gusty west wind. The day that followed was scenic, enjoyable and tough with much pathless boggy terrain. I'd needed that twelve-hour sleep. The early walking along the Kilsyth Hills wasn't too hard and the views across the Central Lowlands were extensive, especially from Leckett Hill and Holehead. I also had views north to higher, more rugged hills: the Highlands! I would be there soon. Between the two tops I crossed a minor road by the source of the River Carron and then the Watershed began to swing north. On Holehead a big white ball sitting on a green box with solar panels below it loomed up: a Met Office weather station.

The first difficulties came after Holehead when I entered the forest and had to negotiate a steep descent through little crags. For once there wasn't a break in the trees, so it was a bit of a struggle. Steep-sided rugged little Dungoil poked out of the trees and was the most interesting hill of the day. Then it was back into the forest again. As the Watershed swung east to round the headwaters of the Endrick Water I crossed the minor road again, only 3 km or so further along. Walking along the tarmac would have saved me a couple of hours' hard work, but I wouldn't have been on the Watershed or enjoyed the challenge, the contact with nature, and the feeling of being immersed in the landscape.

Another overgrown track in dense trees led over Gartcarron Hill where I camped in the forest just east of the top. After ten hours and 19 km I felt tired and this seemed a placid spot to spend the night, quiet and sheltered from the strengthening wind. There was a tiny trickle of a burn, the first I'd seen in a while. It was enough. The abandoned track was stony under the long grass and the pegs went in only just enough to stay in place. A strong gust of wind and the tarp would collapse. But I was surrounded by dense spruce forest and felt secure.

I was woken by lovely bird song – at 3.30 a.m.! It was still going on when I woke again several hours later. I'm not an early riser. I walked down through the forest to the Carron Valley Reservoir. Mostly this was a spruce and larch plantation but the edges of tracks and rides were softened by deciduous trees, especially willows. The big reservoir, which has dams at both ends, fills the valley with the mostly forested hills rising directly from the water. The reservoir was constructed in the 1930s to provide water for the Stirling and Falkirk areas. Eighty years later it's a peaceful lake popular for fishing and birdwatching – there are ospreys though I didn't see one – and many walks on its banks and in the forests. After crossing the dam at the western end, a forest track took me up through the trees to open boggy moorland and the sight of a wind farm on Hart Hill. The turbines were spinning fast in the cold gusty wind that had me reaching for extra clothing once I was out of the trees. The loop round the source of the River Carron was complete now and I was heading northwards to the steep imposing escarpment that runs along the northern edge of the Campsie Fells. In the midst of this rough moorland, dotted with large patches of cotton grass, I felt as remote from towns and roads as almost anywhere on the walk. I saw nobody all day.

After passing the bright lozenges of the Earlsburn Reservoirs I reached the escarpment edge at an ancient cairn named Carleatheran. From here I looked down to the broad valley of the River Forth. To round the headwaters of this I would have to walk west for some 25 km. Across the valley I could see the dark silhouettes of the Trossachs hills. I could have been there in a few hours in a straight line.

My route turned west though, for a wonderful walk along the top of the escarpment. Dark clouds raced across the sky, torn ragged by the strong wind. Crags fell away to my right, the moorland stretched away to my left. I passed above Black Craig and Standmilane Craig before dipping down to a track and the Spout of Ballochleam (Pass of the Leap) where the Boquhan Burn tumbles down the rocks. A final climb led close by this burn to Stronend where the escarpment turns abruptly south. I paused here, gazing over the land below. Here I would leave the Campsie Fells. Soon I'd be leaving the Central Lowlands too. Stronend comes from the Gaelic *sron*, meaning nose, an appropriate description for this jutting angle in the crags.

The descent from Stronend was steep and somewhat tricky. Picking a way through the rocky and often slippery ground required care. Heavy rain started to fall, which didn't help. I was feeling tired and slow and not quite right, my stomach feeling delicate again. It had been quite a tough day. If the weather had been less stormy I'd have camped on the hills, but I knew I'd have a more restful night if I found somewhere sheltered. I was to be glad of this decision. Down on flatter land I found a pleasant dell with a little burn running through it on the edge of Balgair Muir. There was no wind down here and I was out of sight. A scattering of trees and bushes grew along the steep banks of the burn. The rich creamy flowers of hawthorn and the bright yellow of gorse were a welcome sight after the harsh moorland.

Despite the sheltered site, gusts of wind bringing heavy rain woke me several times during the night, which was the wettest and stormiest of the walk so far. I did not feel very well when I finally woke on a grey gloomy morning. I looked at the map. Not far away was the little village of Balfron, and sitting in a café sounded appealing. After a few hours in the wind and rain I was doing just that, still feeling unwell and not a little sorry for myself. A tasty lunch of leek and potato soup in Doyles Café lightened my mood but I still felt tired and shaky and not up to walking much further. A warm and dry night indoors seemed a good idea, but there was nowhere to stay in Balfron. I rang home. Denise realised from my voice that I wasn't well and offered to find the nearest accommodation as it would be much easier for her to do so on the Internet from home than by me on a shaky phone connection. Not long afterwards she texted to say she'd booked me into the Loaninghead B&B, which was only a few km away. It also turned out to be virtually on the Watershed. The convenience of the Internet!

I walked to Loaninghead in the rain, glad to know it wasn't far and that once there I had nothing to do. The B&B was luxurious, which was just what I needed. 'A nice rather grand place', I wrote in my journal. My stomach being upset again, I had no dinner other than a pot of yoghurt and lots of water. I washed myself and my clothes, lay on the bed reading and writing and unwinding, hoping I'd feel better the next day (which I did).

The next morning I was happy to have breakfast in the big ornate dining room, which boasted a large chandelier. The table was set with delicate willow pattern china and cut-glass tumblers. After days eating out of one cookpot and drinking out of the other this seemed quite decadent. After a superb breakfast of muesli and fruit, boiled eggs, toast and marmalade plus lots of excellent coffee – 'best of trip so far', I noted – I felt up to another day's walking. My waterproofs and shoes were dry too, having been taken away by my hosts to a warm room. The shoes came back stuffed with newspaper. They hadn't been dry since Cumbernauld. Staying here had been well worthwhile. The rain had cleared up too.

My shoes didn't stay dry long. The following day was mostly spent on boggy terrain. Wearing light trail shoes mostly made from mesh I didn't expect my feet to stay dry for long unless the weather and the ground were both dry. I find such shoes very comfortable though, much more than boots. I like the flexibility and the contact with the ground. Wet feet weren't a problem as it was never very cold and I could dry them each night.

Shortly after leaving Loaninghead I climbed very gradually up boggy moorland on the start of an extremely long approach to Ben Lomond. The huge Loch Ard Forest gradually began to appear on my right. This part of the Queen Elizabeth Forest Park includes areas of semi-natural forest as well as plantations. Here, all I could see were ranks of conifers. A few small Sitka spruce grew amongst the heather, from seeds blown by the wind I guessed. Soon the broad island-dotted southern end of Loch Lomond appeared on my left. This lies in the Central Lowlands. The narrow northern section of the loch, which would appear soon, is in the Highlands. The land was changing. The islands and shores of the loch were covered in trees and looked rich and luxurious. The green was that of deciduous trees in early summer, bright and fresh and a big contrast to the dark and sombre conifers of the plantations.

From the first little summit, Bat a'Charchel, I could see Ben Lomond in the distance. A radio tower decorated Bat a'Charchel and a line of pylons ran below it above little Muir

Park Reservoir. Then there was nothing but open moorland. A herd of red deer raced over the moorland, the first of the walk. Soon afterwards I had to climb the first deer fence. Once over Tom na Broc – the hill of the badger – the ground steepened for the final climb to Gualann (the shoulder). This 461-metre summit is undistinguished in itself, but is significant for the Watershed as it lies on the Highland Boundary Fault. As well as this natural feature it also lies on the border of an artificial one, Loch Lomond and the Trossachs National Park. Sixty-eight km of the Watershed lies in this, Scotland's first national park.

The Highland Boundary Fault runs across Scotland from the south-west, where it splits the island of Arran in two, to Stonehaven in the north-east. It makes a distinctive line recognisable on the ground in most places. North of the line the landscape is mountainous and rugged, south of it lie gentle moorlands and flat farmland, the country of the Central Lowlands I'd been walking through for the past nine days. The underlying geology is the reason for this difference. North of the fault the rocks are metamorphic schist and slates, to the south they're softer sedimentary sandstones with basalt lava flows forming the few crags and more distinctive hills. The walk was about to change, and I felt that I was returning home.

From Gualann I could see the Highland Boundary Fault as I looked across Loch Lomond. Four islands lie on the line of the Fault – Inchcailloch, Torrinch, Creinch, and Inchmurrin. Turning I could see it in the other direction too, as a line of wooded bumps in the forest – Lime Hill, Maol Ruadh, Drum of Clashmore, and Arndrum. Delineations between regions are not often so clear and obvious.

Before stepping into the Highlands I thought back on my days following the Watershed through the Central Lowlands.

My fears had been unfounded. Whilst there were sections of farmland, roads and buildings, and of course Cumbernauld, most of the walking had been in semi-wild and surprisingly remote-feeling countryside. I'd seen few other people. There'd been no problems finding pleasant places to camp. There'd been much wildlife too, far more than in the Southern Uplands, and a far greater mix of habitats and terrain than I'd been expecting. I was heartened too by the signs of restoration of the now abandoned mining areas. 'A gentle wildness' Peter Wright calls it. I think he's right.

Turning my back on the Lowlands I looked ahead to Ben Lomond, the highest hill by far I'd yet encountered on the walk. Now for the Highlands.

4

STORMY WEATHER TO
THE GREAT GLEN

From Gualann the long broad ridge became steeper and more rugged. There was a mountainous feel I hadn't had since the Southern Uplands. To the north the rugged pyramid of Ben Lomond, the most southerly Munro, stood out as the most dramatic peak I'd seen yet. The nature of the walk was certainly changing.

Ben Lomond is one of the most popular summits in the Highlands, being easily reached from Glasgow. It's a fine peak too. There was, though, no sign anyone came up this long southerly ridge that runs some 12 km from Gualann to the summit, a shame as the views are superb and, although there's no path, the walking is easy. A series of tops led me towards Ben Lomond. I wasn't planning on the summit on this first day in the Highlands, not wanting to push myself too far after the illness of the day before. For the first time in five days my stomach felt fine. I'd eaten normally, walking hadn't seemed an effort, and I wanted to keep it that way. My first camp in the Highlands was a few km before the summit beside the Glashlet Burn. It was a peaceful scenic site, out in the open with extensive views on all sides. The evening was quiet and cloudy, which brought out the midges, so I was soon in my shelter poring over maps and wondering about the hills to come.

I knew the forty-four Munros along the Watershed quite well, having climbed all of them several times, often on long walks (including all the Munros and subsidiary Tops in 1996), but there were still sides of them I'd never walked and this was often where the Watershed ran. At times I'd coincide with the main paths to the summits but often I'd be approaching or descending from hills on rough pathless terrain. This, I thought, would be interesting.

The first eight lie in Loch Lomond and the Trossachs National Park, and the Watershed runs right through its heart. Since its inception in 2002 the park has done much to conserve and enhance the natural beauty and biodiversity of the area, often in partnership with landowning bodies such as the National Trust for Scotland, the RSPB, and the Woodland Trust. This is what national parks should be for. Unfortunately, the park authority has become embroiled in unnecessary controversies that detract from the good work it is doing. Due to some damage being done by some campers along the road on the east side of Loch Lomond, the park decided to use a sledgehammer and instituted a camping ban which was now beginning. Since then the bye-laws have been extended to many other loch shores in the park.

Given that the access legislation allows for access rights to be removed if people don't follow the Outdoor Access Code there is no need for this legislation. Dealing with those involved in damage could have been done without a blanket ban that penalises everybody. It just required enforcement of the access legislation. High above the loch I was well above the camping ban area, but I still felt concerned, aware that below me a tired walker on the West Highland Way, Scotland's most popular long-distance path, which runs beside the loch, might be wondering whether they should camp and risked being fined. This is not what park rangers should be doing.

Another controversy concerns a gold mine on the slopes of Ben Lui, which I would reach in the next week, hoping to see what was going on. Mining in a national park seemed a bad idea. I'd seen the remnants of gold mines many years before when I'd walked through the Klondike area of the Yukon Territory in Canada, and I knew that the scars take a long time to heal.

Sunshine heating the Trailstar woke me next morning. The temperature was 20°C and I was far too hot in my sleeping bag. I had breakfast outside. My first full day in the Highlands was starting well. Not far from camp I joined the well-worn, standard route up Ben Lomond from Rowardennan on Loch Lomond. Many walkers were heading up, more than I'd seen in total on the whole walk so far. I joined the throng. The views were superb, especially down to Loch Lomond and across to the rugged peaks of the Arrochar Alps with the distinctive profile of The Cobbler standing out.

For the first time I was on a summit in the company of many others. Ben Lomond deserves its popularity. The little rocky top is in a superb situation with dizzying views down to the loch. Unsurprisingly for a hill so clearly in view from the Central Lowlands, Ben Lomond was one of the first Highland summits to become popular with recreational walkers. The first recorded ascent was in 1758.

The name is often said to mean beacon hill, from the old British 'llumon'. Standing out as it does, the name would be appropriate. Peter Drummond reckons it might also come from the Gaelic *luimean*, a bare hill, due to its treeless summit rising above wooded slopes.

Leaving the summit I headed a short way down the rocky Ptarmigan Ridge before turning down the long north ridge. The other walkers vanished suddenly. I saw no-one else all day. There were no paths. I circled the head of Gleann Gaoithe and then turned east along little boggy hills. The air was calm and humid and whenever I paused clouds of midges rose up. All afternoon it was peat bog after peat bog alongside a deer fence. There were many deer on this quieter side of Ben Lomond. Pale pink and purple orchids grew in the boggy areas and the drier ground was dotted with yellow tormentil. For the last few hours I followed a new and more intrusive deer fence, finally finding a gate near a line of pylons and a minor road. I camped not far away, near the end of Loch Arklet. A cuckoo called incessantly as I made supper. It had been a tough day.

The night was warm and muggy. I woke, feeling sticky, to the sound of raindrops on the tarp and the cuckoo still calling. By the time I set off the rain was heavy and constant, which at least meant the midges had retreated. The Watershed between Loch Arklet and Loch Katrine is just 500 metres wide. I was now in the Trossachs, an area of lake and forest that is softer than most of the Highlands and which always reminds me of the English Lake District. The name originally referred only to the land between the eastern end of Loch Katrine and Loch Achray. It comes from the Gaelic *Na Troiseachan*, meaning the crossing place. Peter Drummond says this probably means that boats could be dragged across the low land between the two lochs. Today the name 'Trossachs' is used for the much larger area all around Loch Katrine.

The Trossachs is a favourite tourist spot for the people of Glasgow and the surrounding area, popularised in the nineteenth century by Sir Walter Scott in his poem *The Lady of the Lake* (the lake being Loch Katrine) and the novel *Rob Roy*. Today, one of the last steam-powered passenger ships in Britain, the SS Sir Walter Scott carries tourists up and down the loch as it has done for over a hundred years.

Setting off in the rain I had to admit my main interest in Loch Katrine was the thought of the Pier Tea Room at Stronachlachar. In a boggy area close to my camp a bright red Forestry Commission sign read 'No unauthorised persons beyond this point'. The thick vegetation looked the same either side of the sign. I ignored it. A prolonged second break-fast that merged into an early lunch kept me in the Tea Room for two and a half hours. Procrastination is useful when it's raining and you're somewhere nice and warm with hot drinks and tasty food. Waiting to see if the rain stopped and then walking into the evening or even the night could lead to a more enjoyable day. At least that's what I told myself as I kept putting off starting out again. Outside, the grey waters of the loch faded into distant cloud-capped hills. The shores were lined with mixed woodland, rich, green and dripping.

The delay was vindicated when the rain ceased. The skies were still grey when I left the café but there was now a breeze so the midges had gone. From Stronachlachar the Watershed goes straight up a steep little hill called Garradh. The ascent was brutal, a very steep climb through soaking wet, waist-high bracken. Once the summit was reached the walking became easier with gentler slopes and no bracken. Looking back, I could see the two lochs, Katrine and Arklet, and the narrow neck between them. Views like this always brought home the reality of the Watershed. The rain that had just fallen would end up in either the North Sea or the Atlantic Ocean depending on where it fell. Down on Loch Katrine tiny Sir Walter Scott left a huge V-shaped wake as it steamed along the water.

From Garradh a rugged ridge ran above the lochs to the fine pointed Corbett Beinn a'Choin (hill of the dog). The clouds were rising now and there were craggy hills all around. A ptarmigan, grey against the rocks, fluttered low over the ground. From a marshy col a snipe zigzagged into the air. There were many deer and one goat, a shaggy black billy with huge horns, one of them half-broken. He watched me as I passed, unconcerned, before going back to grazing. Amongst the tangle of fresh blueberry leaves and rough grasses the white star flowers of chickweed wintergreen sparkled. There were no paths and no other walkers.

From Beinn a'Choin I looked back over the Watershed, following its twisting line all the way to now distant Ben Lomond. I never tired of tracing its line over the hills. Doing so really gave me a feel for how the land was made. My mind went back beyond Ben Lomond, back over the Central Lowlands, and along the Southern Uplands to Peel Fell. The thread linking it all together. I had, I realised, already come a long way.

Whilst the scene was mostly one of wild rugged grandeur, the line of pylons I'd camped near were always in sight, paralleling the Watershed alongside Loch Katrine and up Glen Gyle. Above the head of that glen I passed under them again. I was now approaching the four Munros above Glen Falloch. I camped on a windy col below the first, Beinn Chabhair, under a bright half-moon.

The walk over the four Munros – Beinn Chabhair, An Caisteal, Beinn a'Chroin and Cruach Ardrain – was rough and rocky with much ascent and descent. The weather was becoming wilder with showers and an increasingly strong south-west wind. The clouds stayed above the tops though, so the views were tremendous. There was no path between Beinn Chabhair and An Caisteal and I had to search around for a route up the craggy face of the latter (the name means 'The Castle') eventually finding a way via a steep grassy gully. On An Caisteal a good path appeared, along with the first walkers I'd seen since Ben Lomond, one of them on his 50th Munro.

Beyond Beinn a'Chroin the path continued, the other walkers didn't, and I had the climb up Cruach Ardrain, the first 1,000-metre summit of the walk, to myself. The wind was now fierce, and I was glad I had no more hills to climb that day. I looked southwards. I was now about to leave the catchment area of the River Forth which I'd joined all those days ago in the Pentland Hills. From here on, only the Watershed would connect me with the Central Lowlands. A part of the journey was over. Not far away I could see the distinctive twin pyramids of Ben More and Stob Binnein. These lie east of the Watershed though, so I turned away to follow a long ridge down into conifer forest and the little village of Crianlarich, which is just half a kilometre from the Watershed.

It was eight days since I'd last had a break from walking, and that was when I was being ill in Cumbernauld. With a long section coming up I'd always planned on a rest day in Crianlarich. First, I needed somewhere to stay and that proved difficult as everywhere was full, the summer season being well under way. I never like booking accommodation far in advance – deadlines take away some of the feeling of freedom. I didn't want the pressure of having to push on if I didn't feel like it. The penalty for that approach was sometimes finding there was nowhere to stay but I preferred to take that risk.

Eventually I found a room in the youth hostel, which was fine for the night but not for the next day. I wanted a base where I could come and go, and the Y.H. was shut for most of the day. I had an enjoyable evening chatting to the warden who'd twice walked across Scotland on The Great Outdoors Challenge, a backpacking event organised every year by *The Great Outdoors* magazine, in the early 1980s as I had done, though we didn't remember if we'd met. He had a copy of my guidebook to walks on the Isle of Skye which I signed.

71

The Ben More Hotel had mentioned they might have a room free the next night. I arrived in time for breakfast. They had; a little wooden lodge, and let me move in straight away. Outside it was dull with drizzle, and I was quite happy not to be walking. The forecast was concerning though. In two days a really big storm with savage winds and torrential rain was meant to arrive. I collected my next set of maps from the Post Office and studied them. Rugged high hills and a complex route lay ahead for quite some way. If the winds made walking difficult or even dangerous what would I do? I didn't want to spend several days sitting out a storm, but I knew that going over the Munros in really bad weather was unwise even in summer. Twice on my Munros and Tops walk I'd been driven down by the wind. Staying dry and navigating in heavy rain and minimal visibility weren't a problem. I'd done that many times before – so often that I no longer found it a challenge. Knock-you-over winds were a different matter though. I'd been lifted off my feet a few times in the past. I'd never suffered more than a few bruises, but I knew I could easily have broken bones. There was a limit to how much risk I was prepared to take.

The day in Crianlarich revolved around the Ben More Hotel and the Station Tea Room. A visit to the small store produced supplies for the next six or so days. The choice was limited. On long walks I've always preferred to buy food as I've gone along rather than sending supply boxes. Again, one reason is the freedom it gives. I'm not dependent on boxes arriving nor on reaching places when Post Offices are open. Against that, I had to eat what was available. Here that meant instant noodles, instant potato powder, instant soup, and pasta sauce mixes for dinners, sugar-rich muesli for breakfast, oatcakes, cheese in tubes and lots of boiled sweets and chocolate and flapjack for the constant snacks that constituted lunch. Not the healthiest diet but it would keep me going.

Crianlarich is an important village for walkers. It lies on the West Highland Way and is surrounded by Munros. I'd resupplied here on my Land's End to John o'Groats walk in 1978 and my Munros and Tops walk in 1996, staying here on the latter too. Crianlarich is also on the West Highland Line and on other occasions I'd come here by train. I like it.

From Crianlarich the Watershed heads west to the Ben Lui hills. I crossed the West Highland Way where a stream of heavily laden walkers (much bigger packs than mine) were heading north. I saw no-one else all day. Even in the Highlands the Watershed was proving quite lonely. This approach to the three Munros of the Ben Lui group is lengthy and I spent a few hours going over little-frequented pathless tops before I reached the first of them, Beinn Dubhcraig. Golden plover called plaintively and herds of deer raced away.

The day had been cloudy, but the skies cleared as I reached the summit of Beinn Dubhcraig to give a superb view over the hills to distant Loch Lomond and Ben Lomond. The light was glorious. For half an hour. Then the clouds covered the sun and the brightness faded, but that view had been magnificent and sent me off to the next Munro, Ben Oss, feeling exhilarated and energetic. After crossing the latter I camped on the col below Ben Lui with the wind picking up. It started to rain as I fell asleep.

The big storm came in just before midnight with 'ridiculously heavy rain' and very strong winds that shook the Trailstar violently. I didn't think it would collapse but I also didn't think I would get any sleep with the noise and movement. Reluctantly I donned waterproofs on my bare skin and staggered outside in bare feet. In the dark and mist and rain I dragged the tarp with all my belongings bundled in it a little way downhill and pitched it again. The winds strengthened. I got out and repeated the process. I was now only about 50 metres from where I'd first camped but the difference was enormous. Here the hillside sheltered me from much of the wind. Tired now I slept well, waking occasionally to the sound of heavy rain. It was still hammering down the next morning and I dawdled over several mugs of coffee, happy to stay in the dry. The barometer on my little portable weather meter showed the lowest pressure of the trip so far.

Eventually I hauled myself out into the rain and packed up. Often when you do this it turns out not to be so bad outside after all. That wasn't the case on this occasion. The rain and wind were both fierce, and dense cloud shrouded the hills. A good path led up Ben Lui where four others stood by the summit cairn, the only people I saw all day. They were going on to the fourth Munro in this group, Beinn a'Chleibh. It's not on the Watershed so I watched them disappear into the mist before starting down the north side of Ben Lui.

The descent was horrible. There was no path and there were many little crags to weave a way through. Minimal visibility meant I often couldn't see ways down and went back and forth along slippery grassy shelves above the crags until I found a safe descent. Progress was slow and difficult, and I needed to concentrate. A slip here could result in a nasty accident. When the angle finally eased I felt very relieved. With the storm behind me, the wind blasted me along to another Corbett, Beinn Chuirn, and then lower Meall Odhar. I saw nothing until early evening when the clouds parted slightly, and a series of rainbows brightened the greyness. I had glimpses of the peaks around me and then the rain and mist closed in again. Occasionally, startled deer raced off into the clouds and at one point a big mountain hare watched me pass. At a col I found a reasonably sheltered spot and made camp. It had been a tough but slow day. Twelve km had taken me nine hours.

Wind and rain woke me early. The storm had strengthened again. On 590-metre Sron nan Colan, just above my camp, the wind was gusting to 30mph, the speed at which walking starts to become difficult. Higher up it would be much stronger. Walking down from this little summit through large areas of old, gold mining, debris (I saw nothing of the new mine or the effect it's having on the landscape) to the village of Tyndrum I pondered my options. There were big hills to come. I needed a weather forecast. Once in the shelter of the The Green Welly Stop Restaurant I checked the Mountain Weather Information Service (MWIS). Gusts of wind up to 65mph and continuing rain. The hills to come were steep and exposed. I'd climbed them all several times before. Did I want to do so again in a big storm? No. But it was where the Watershed went. I had a decision to make.

My plan had always been to follow the Watershed as closely as possible but not to do so absolutely if conditions suggested it would be miserable or even dangerous. The weather forecast for the next few days suggested both. I could have waited the stormy weather out in Tyndrum, but I knew that another storm might closely follow, and I didn't want to take days off now anyway. I was feeling strong and like moving on every day. I looked at the maps. There was an obvious alternative route, the West Highland Way, which intersected the Watershed twice north of Tyndrum beyond the next section of high hills. Going this way would keep the walk continuous but would miss two mountainous sections.

I thought about why I was doing this walk. To get a feel for the Watershed on the ground, to enjoy being out for weeks at a time, to experience nature and wild places. Staggering over rain and wind lashed hills, seeing nothing, didn't fit any of those. I already knew that when I couldn't see the Watershed stretching out I lost contact with it and could have been anywhere. The challenge of surviving storms high in the hills no longer appealed to me. I'd done it too often. I wanted to enjoy the walk. The West Highland Way it would be.

I took the approach of the Continental Divide Trail which I'd walked from Canada to Mexico along the Rocky Mountains nearly thirty years earlier. That route is sometimes on the actual watershed of the USA but more often it parallels it on lower, easier terrain. I'd still gained a feel for the Continental Divide, still felt it as a high line running the length of the country. I hoped it would be the same here.

This was to be the furthest I strayed from the Watershed. I knew it was there, up in the invisible hills, and I knew I'd be re-joining it soon, but for now I was abandoning it. Once the decision was made I felt relief, which told me it was the right one. I really hadn't wanted to struggle through mist and rain battered by the wind. Every long-distance walker sets their own aims. 'HYOH – Hike Your Own Hike' as American long-distance hikers say. There are no absolute rules.

My aim on every walk has always been to walk the whole way, without a break, from start to finish without jumping ahead to find easier terrain or avoid bad weather and then returning to complete the missed section later. Only on my Munros and Tops walk had I felt constrained. The whole point of that walk was to climb every single summit, so that's what I did, though sometimes the weather drove me down and I had to go back the next day to collect missed peaks. I could have skipped ahead now and done a lower section in the stormy weather and then come back and done the hills here in better weather, but that would have been breaking the walk in a way that taking a route below the Watershed didn't. Continuity mattered. The Watershed was a continuous line. I wanted my walk to be one too, even if in places I wasn't on the Watershed itself. Such are the decisions long-distance walkers sometimes have to make!

The West Highland Way was familiar territory. I'd first followed the route on my Land's End to John o'Groats walk, two years before it was officially opened. There'd been no signposts, no well-worn path, no facilities for walkers back then. Now this 155-km path, which runs from Milngavie on the outskirts of Glasgow to finish below Ben Nevis at Fort William, is one of the most popular long-distance paths. Fifteen thousand people are reckoned to walk the whole length every year. Many thousands more walk sections of it. I hadn't walked it in full again but I had walked sections on many long-distance walks. It's often maligned by more experienced walkers as rather dull, but I think that's unfair. It passes through some magnificent country and makes a good introduction to long-distance walking.

In 2010 the West Highland Way became the first European section of the International Appalachian Trail (IAT), an ambitious undertaking to continue the Appalachian Trail in the USA north through Canada and then via Greenland to Scotland, Ireland, Scandinavia and Spain, linking areas that were part of the Caledonian Mountain range some 480–390 million years ago but were torn apart when the Atlantic Ocean formed about 150 million years ago. A year earlier I'd accompanied people from Canada and the UK involved with setting up the IAT on a walk over Ben Nevis and Carn Mor Dearg. As well as the trail itself the IAT has the very laudable aim 'to promote natural and cultural heritage, health and fitness, environmental stewardship, fellowship and understanding, cross-border cooperation, and rural economic development through eco and geo tourism'. I was to think of this as I passed IAT signs in the next two days and wondered what other walkers thought of seeing them.

In Tyndrum I learnt from a walker called Jeff, who turned out to be a Facebook contact, that I'd just missed the annual West Highland Way Race. There was a new astonishing record of just over 15 hours (since then it's been broken again and now stands at 13 hours 40 minutes). Not moving anything like as fast as the runners, I managed the 12km to Bridge of Orchy in two hours and wrote in my journal: 'the joys of a good path!' I was covering ground much faster than I had for many days. The weather stayed very windy and overcast with the clouds low down on the hills. There were few other walkers – most had probably finished their day earlier. I had a meal in the Bridge of Orchy Hotel then strode on into the evening, crossing the Watershed where it cut back west before heading into the Black Mount hills, before camping on the edge of Rannoch Moor.

A tent I passed was the first other wild camp I'd seen on the walk. The two people there had a lit a fire. They were heading south along the West Highland Way and said there was no wood to the north. I wasn't planning on a fire anyway. They looked to be using a well-established fire ring. I hoped they wouldn't leave any mess, which is too often the result of camp fires in wild places.

As I packed up the next morning two more walkers passed me, both on mobile phones, one talking, one staring at the screen. Maybe they were fed up with the scenery and the sounds of nature. The wind was still strong and cold but the clouds had lifted a little and the light was lovely as the sun cut through in shafts of brightness. Ahead was the great rock pyramid of the Buachaille Etive Mor. There were flowers by the track: the tiny pink flower mats of moss campion, the nodding purple bells of common butterwort rising on a slender stem above the roseate of sticky insect-catching leaves.

Breakfast was in the Glencoe Mountain Café, after barely an hour's walk. There was a campsite here too. Nice to have facilities, I thought, but I preferred my wild site. Other walkers were setting off, all with much bigger packs than mine. I wondered what they were carrying.

Ahead of me lay some of the grandest hills in the Highlands, the magnificent Glencoe mountains, the splendid long ridges of the Mamores and the Grey Corries, Ben Nevis itself. I was to turn away from these wonderful mountains though, for here the Watershed takes what seems a strange direction, heading east over much lower hills on the northern edge of Rannoch Moor. I was as close to those West Highland hills as the Watershed comes. They're all well to the west. It was the continuous high line again, not the highest hills, that I was following.

Before re-joining the Watershed itself, I continued along the West Highland Way to the Kingshouse Hotel where I had a panini and orange juice for an early lunch. I resisted having beer as I wanted to walk much further and feared it might make me sleepy. There were many West Highland Way walkers in the bar, with a row of their mobile phones jostling for charging sockets along a shelf, and some tents pitched outside.

The Kingshouse has long played a major role in Scottish mountaineering and hillwalking. Set dramatically below Buachaille Etive Mor, whose cliffs have been a major climbing area since the birth of mountaineering in Scotland, it is far from any other hotels or bars. Dating from the 1740s it began life as a coaching inn and a stopover for drovers taking cattle to markets in the south. In the early days it seems to have survived on its remoteness rather than the quality of accommodation or food. The Wordsworths stayed here in 1803 and Dorothy described it as 'a wretched place' while as late as the

1930s the climber J. H. B. Bell described it as 'still primitive' and said that there were holes in the floors and the roof leaked. However, not long afterwards W. H. Murray, author of the wonderful *Mountaineering in Scotland*, used it as a base and was full of praise. I'd first visited the Kingshouse on my Land's End to John o'Groats walk and had been back quite a few times since and enjoyed every visit.

From the Kingshouse an old rough vehicle track led to the cluster of buildings at Black Corries Lodge. Here I finally re-joined the Watershed, having crossed it earlier en route to the café – the temptations of breakfast inside out of the cold wind having been too much to resist, as then had the thought of lunch in the Kingshouse. A curiosity along the way to Black Corries was a large blue plastic barrel mounted on a wooden tripod and surrounded by a circle of wire netting on the edge of a small fenced copse. 'Rajah Brand Curry Paste Mild' it said on the side, 'Product of India', along with a long list of ingredients and the weight 55,000kg. That's an awful lot of curry!

A spout under the barrel was full of pellets of some kind. I guessed it was now a feeder for red grouse, to keep them fat and healthy so they could be shot. Black Corries is a shooting estate (I don't like the word 'sporting' for such estates as I see nothing sporting about blasting birds out of the sky with shotguns or killing deer with high-powered rifles) and lists grouse as one of the victims.

From Black Corries I was disappointed to see that the old path, which I remembered using many years earlier, had been replaced by an ugly, wide new bulldozed road that ended after 3 km in a huge turning circle. Looking back, I could see the pale scar of the track cutting through the landscape like a slash across a painting. Beyond this desecration Buachaille Etive Mor and surrounding peaks were dark against swirling

1. Peter Wright on the way to Peel Fell

2. The first day, on Peel Fell in mist and rain

6. The Grey Mare's Tail and Loch Skeen

BE YE MAN OR WUMMAN
BE YE SUIN OR LATE
BE YE GAEIN OR COMIN
BE SHAIR TAE SHUT THIS GATE

Beware
of bull

TOP LEFT:

7. Tussocks, plantations and wind turbines. Tony Hobbs on the Watershed in the Southern Uplands

TOP RIGHT:

8. I think that's clear!

LEFT:

9. The Watershed in the Central Lowlands feels surprisingly remote

12. Wind farm in the Central Lowlands

13. St Katherine's Well

14. The line of the Antonine Wall

15. The Forth and Clyde Canal

16. Looking back to Loch Lomond from the ascent of Ben Lomond

TOP LEFT:

17. The Watershed crosses
the West Highland Way near
Crianlarich

TOP RIGHT:

18. View back to Loch Lomond
and Ben Lomond from Beinn
Dubhcraig

LEFT:

19. A rainbow brightens the sky
after the storm on Ben Lui

20. International Appalachian Trail sign along the West Highland Way

21. Ugly bulldozed track near the Black Corries and Rannoch Moor

22. View across Rannoch Moor from Stob na Cruaiche

Dunan

1ˢᵗ August – 20ᵗʰ October

For safety could you please keep to the marked routes between these dates.

Please keep all dogs on a lead

If you have any queries please ring: 07881718233

Thank you for your co-operation

23. Signs like this don't conform with the access legislation

26. In the Great Glen

Top left:

30. Fences divide the land.
Inside, trees and heather.
Outside, bog

Left:

31. After a wild night. Camp at
Loch a'Bhealaich

Top Right:

32. Jonathan outside Maol
Bhuidhe bothy

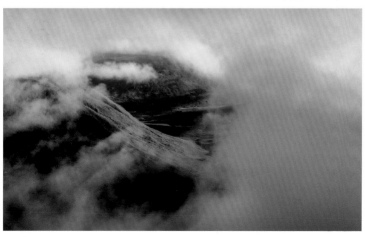

ABOVE:

33. Slioch, Lochan Fada and the Fisherfield hills

LEFT:

34. A hole in the clouds. In the Fannichs

35. In the Fannichs

36. Gleann na Squaib from the ascent of Beinn Dearg

37. A chance meeting with another Watershed walker. David Edgar on Beinn Leoidh

ABOVE:

38. Shafts of sunlight, Loch Choire

BELOW:

39. The spread of technology. Signs
in the Flow Country

40. View across the Flow Country to Morven

41. Camp in the vast expanse of the Flow Country

42. Almost there. The stacks of Duncansby with the Lighthouse in the distance

43. Finished! Duncansby Head.

clouds split by spears of sunlight, dramatic and monochrome. Squalls of rain raced across the hills.

As I climbed, splendid views opened up across the vast loch-strewn expanse of Rannoch Moor to the hills above Bridge of Orchy, the Watershed hills I'd passed in the storm. Now they were free of cloud and rain though the wind still tore through the sky and was strong on the much lower hills I was now traversing. Where the sun pierced the clouds, the moor shone bright green and blue, the grasses glowing, the water shining. At its heart two long lochs, Ba and Laidon, stretched across the land.

Rannoch Moor seems an anomaly. What is such a huge flat area doing in the midst of the mountains? In fact, the centre of the last great ice sheet to cover the Highlands was here, with the ice at its thickest. From Rannoch Moor the ice radiated in all directions, its courses now marked by streams and rivers. Once the moor was wooded, as evidenced by the many decaying tree stumps. Now it's a classic blanket peat bog.

Free of the horrible new road I followed a very old overgrown track to Stob nan Losgann and then Stob na Cruaiche, the highest summit on this long line of undulating hills, whose name means, appropriately, 'Peak of the Peat Stack'. From the summit the ring of mountains around Rannoch Moor make up the horizon. Beyond the summit the Watershed starts a long descent over lower tops towards the east end of Loch Laidon. In places I found double lines of fences laid horizontally where the track crossed boggy areas, giving a corduroy effect as they ran across the hillside. I'd never seen this before. I walked into the evening as the light changed and the sky was a mass of wonderful shades of blues, pinks and whites with the mountains golden in the sun or black under the clouds. Far to the south-east the cone of Schiehallion stood out.

Once I was down in the forest above Loch Laidon, and out of the wind, the midges appeared, clouds of them if I stopped for even a second. Setting up camp would be horrific with so many swarming round my head. I pushed on. Pink lines of cloud streaked across the sky. Buildings appeared, Rannoch Station on the West Highland Line, and also the Moor of Rannoch Hotel. I went in. Yes, they had a room and could provide dinner despite my late arrival at 9.30 p.m. The small hotel was friendly and comfortable, the dinner excellent. I celebrated a long enjoyable day with a bottle of excellent beer – Harviestoun's Schiehallion, of course.

The Moor of Rannoch had no Wi-Fi or mobile coverage, which was fine with me. I was happy not to be tempted into connecting with the world outside. There were no radios or TVs either. Breakfast was peaceful and excellent and 'second only to Loaninghead' as I wrote in my journal. I didn't note what I ate other than 'lovely yoghurt' – it must have really impressed me. Outside the window, deer grazed in a butter-cup-and-daisy-dotted meadow.

Tearing myself away from the quiet and peace of The Moor of Rannoch I headed back to the Watershed. The sky was still overcast, with rain looking likely, but the wind had lessened greatly and that was the key to walking high up being enjoyable rather than a struggle. In *Ribbon of Wildness*, Peter Wright, who walked the Watershed in a series of trips, says he wanted 'to avoid the risk of being overwhelmed by the notion of one big long, and perhaps unremitting trek'. I'd opted for the big, long trek but I did want to avoid the unre-mitting part. Not fighting along the Watershed in big storms was my way of doing that. Today though, the hill tops looked a good place to be and I was to make the most of this, follow-ing the Watershed over seven summits, three of them Munros. The north-west wind was cold but never strong enough to impede walking. The clouds stayed above the tops and only brought rain late in the day.

The Watershed turns north-east here, heading for its furthest point from the Atlantic Ocean in the Highlands, though the North Sea is still much further away. Scotland is tilted to the east so the Watershed doesn't run down the centre of the country, as you might expect, but is generally on the western side. Sometimes, as I would soon experience, it's actually west of inlets of the Atlantic Ocean. Here the north-east trend away from the Atlantic is unusual, the only time this occurs in the Highlands.

The Watershed lay on a long, undulating and quite broad but steep-sided ridge between Loch Ossian and the giant reservoir of Loch Ericht. I followed this over a series of hills, including the Munros Carn Dearg and Sgor Gaibhre. The views were dark and flat under the clouds, with hills fading into insubstantiality and nothing really standing out. Back west over Rannoch Moor the Blackwater Reservoir came into view with the Glencoe peaks beyond, grey silhouettes in this light. Ahead lay the massive bulk of Ben Alder, where I'd be soon, while across Loch Ericht the easily identifiable cone of Schiehallion rose into the sky. There was a sense of space and vastness and, as always, I enjoyed the feeling of being above the world. I enjoyed too, being able to stride out on the stony ground. From all around came the thin piping of golden plover and I had glimpses of these birds gliding low over the sparse grasses or standing on a tussock. Through my binoculars I admired their distinctive speckled gold backs and black fronts. They are birds of wild moorland country and one of my favourites.

Climbing up to the ridge I passed a sign headed 'Dunan', that warned of deer stalking with rifles between 1 August and 20 October and saying 'for safety could you please keep to the marked routes'. I was outside those dates, but I'd have ignored the sign if I had been inside them as this is just the type of notice that was common before the access legislation but which hold no weight now (and never did anyway). Such signs should be removed. Just the sight of this one annoyed me. It was designed to intimidate and put people off going where they liked for almost three months. Information on where stalking is taking place on specific days with requests to avoid those spots is in the spirit of the legislation. Vague threats of being shot are not.

The sign and my feelings about it forgotten, I dropped down steeply to the Bealach Cumhann on the western corner of 1,148-metre Ben Alder, one of the major hills of the Central Highlands and also one of the most remote. It's a massive plateau mountain with steep sides, many of them craggy. The name has nothing to do with alder trees (the Gaelic for alder is *fearna*) but its meaning is unclear. It first appears on early maps as Bin Ailloir and Bin Aildir. Peter Drummond says it may come from ail-dhobhair, meaning water of rock. Whatever the derivation, it's a fine mountain with burns running northwards to the Atlantic Ocean and others running south to the North Sea. The Watershed crosses west to east between these streams.

A long climb took me up grassy slopes past many herds of deer to the plateau, where I was surprised to find large snow beds still remaining, some of which I crossed as I headed for the highest point, which lies on the eastern edge of the mountain. I wasn't expecting to see this much snow in late June. The views were hazier now, with distant mountains disappearing into thickening clouds. I gazed eastwards. Somewhere in that swirling mass, were the Cairngorms, my home hills. If I was to see them on this walk it would be in the next few days. Rain started to fall as I left the summit.

From the top I curved round the edge of the crags of Garbh Choire ('rough corrie' – one of many with this name in the Highlands) to Bealach Breabag. Here I camped, looking down to long Lochan a' Bhealaich Bheithe. I'd walked 27km and been out for over eleven hours. From the bealach the Watershed climbed to another Munro, but that could wait until the next day. I was thinking of hot food and lying down rather than walking further. This was a splendid spot too, with excellent views. At 844 metres it was my highest camp so far.

To the south, a burn descends to Loch Ericht and the bothy of Benalder Cottage, which is often said to be haunted. This comes from a false story about a gamekeeper committing suicide there. I've stayed there quite a few times, usually on my own. Of course there are creaks and noises, as in any bothy, and animals outside can make spooky noises too, but you soon get used to those and, in my case, it probably helps that I live in an old house in the countryside with its own noises and animals inside (bats) and out.

I have experienced some unnerving things in bothies though. Many years ago, in a bothy far from Ben Alder, I was woken by the door latch rattling. I called hello, assuming it was a late arrival. No reply. The rattling stopped for a while, but then began again. I walked quietly to the door then suddenly jerked it open, turning on my headlamp at the same time. A stag sprang back. So did I. I don't know which of us was the most startled. I guess he'd been rubbing his itchy velvet-shedding antlers against the door.

On another occasion in Culra Bothy, not far to the north of Ben Alder, I'd had an even bigger fright. Again I was alone and had just fallen asleep when I was disturbed by a noise. This time it was what sounded like chains being dragged along the outside walls. I sat up, headlamp in hand. Whatever could it be? My brain couldn't find a sensible answer. Soon it would reach the door. I tensed, aiming my lamp at the door. Finally it opened. I switched the lamp on, right into some-one's face. As with the stag I don't know who was more surprised. The explanation was not one I'd have thought of however hard I'd tried. My companion had cycled in on a track from Dalwhinnie station in the evening. At a ford he'd come off his bike and broken his only lamp. Eventually he found the bothy in the dark and then felt his way round the walls searching for the door. The sounds I'd heard were from his bicycle. If one of us had called out we could both have been saved a shock!

Some people do find bothies a little creepy. For a few years I led backpacking trips in the western Highlands for Outward Bound Loch Eil. We mostly camped but, if there was a bothy nearby and it was empty, we used it, especially in stormy weather. One group wouldn't do this, however, saying they couldn't sleep inside one, they were too spooky. Twice on that trip I had a bothy to myself while the group camped nearby. They thought I was very brave. I was just happy to be out of the wind and the rain and the midges.

Not far above Benalder Cottage is a cave said to have been used by Bonnie Prince Charlie in 1746 whilst hiding from troops after defeat at the Battle of Culloden. Charlie is said to have lived in the cave with clan chief Cluny Macpherson for five months. Fictional fugitives came this way too, David Balfour and Alan Breck in Robert Louis Stevenson's *Kidnapped*. Ben Alder doesn't come out well in the novel being described as a 'dismal mountain' with 'dreary glens and hollows'. It's not like that at all!

Lying in my sleeping bag that evening, watching the hills fade into blackness I reflected on the fact that I'd seen no-one all day. That wasn't unusual on the Watershed, as much of it is little-visited and pathless, but today I'd come over three

Munros, one of them, Ben Alder, well known and popular. However, I hadn't been on the latter until the evening and I remembered from my Munros and Tops walk that most folk were on the hills between 9 a.m. and 5 p.m. Outside those hours the hills were often empty. Carn Dearg and Sgor Gaibhre are not very distinctive and I would guess mostly climbed by keen Munro baggers. The paths on those hills had been sketchy.

Being alone in the hills has never bothered me. Indeed, I often prefer it as then I see more wildlife and feel more connected with the land. I'm rarely bored in wild places, there's always so much to see, to think about, to do. Walking is not a repetitive thoughtless activity. Navigation and route-finding (these aren't the same – the first is about the direction you need to go to a destination, the second is about how to get there, which is rarely in a straight line) occupied some time every day, sometimes most of it. Negotiating obstacles – streams, crags, fallen trees, fences – requires thought and care too, but whilst these are interesting the real joy comes from watching the clouds, the birds, the animals, the grasses, the flowers, the whole natural world. I never tire of this, and the next day was to be one of the most satisfying in this regard.

I could see the next Munro from my camp. Beinn Bheoil lay just 2 km away and I was soon on the summit. This long narrow ridge of a mountain lies across Lochan a'Bhealaich Bheithe from Ben Alder and gives tremendous views of the crags and corries of the steep eastern slopes of that hill. It's also a place where I was really aware of being on the Watershed as, below me, I could see both Lochan a' Bhealaich Bheithe and Loch Ericht, whose waters drained to the Atlantic and the North Sea respectively. The narrowness of the Watershed at this point is very clear with steep slopes dropping down to each loch.

Ben Bheoil is close to the easternmost point of the Watershed in the Highlands. It's also the closest the Watershed comes to the centre of Scotland, including the islands, at least according to a centre of gravity method used by the Ordnance Survey. This says that if a cut-out of Scotland is balanced on the tip of a pin then the centre is close to Loch Garry, some 14.5km east of Beinn Bheoil. Leave out the islands, which seems simpler, and by this method the centre is some 5km east of Schiehallion, in which case I'd been at the closest the Watershed comes the day before, just north of Rannoch Station. Of course, all calculations as to the centre of Scotland are approximate as the country is such an irregular shape. Perhaps more significantly for the Watershed, this was the section where it was furthest from either coast. I had a fair way to walk before I was close to the west coast. I'd never come close to the east coast in the Highlands.

From Beinn Bheoil the Watershed descends towards the Allt a'Chaoil-reidhe and Culra Bothy, where I'd had the scare with the night-time cyclist. Asbestos having been found in the walls this bothy is now closed, which is a shame as it's in an excellent situation, ideal for the ascent of many Munros, including Ben Alder.

The Watershed wanders across boggy moorland just east of the Allt a'Chaoil-reidhe. I took the easier option of the track by the burn that leads to Loch Pattack. Sandpipers were bobbing and calling noisily on shingle banks by the water. These distinctive little waders with their contrasting brown uppers and white breasts are common along streams and rivers in the Highlands in summer, and I've always loved hearing them whistling and watching them fly low and stiff-winged along the water's edge before perching on a stone and beginning their nodding again.

Pausing by Loch Pattack I noticed some birds far out on the water. I lifted my binoculars. A family of black-throated divers! I was entranced. The two youngsters were quite large but still downy-looking. As I watched, one of the adults dived and then surfaced with a fish, which it fed to its offspring. Black-throated divers are one of the most magnificent birds of the Highlands. With striking black, grey and white plumage and long pointed beaks they are very distinctive. They're big birds and sit low in the water, their shape often enabling identification from some distance away. They have a haunting call that sends chills down the spine, the epitome of wildness.

The diver family slowly drifted into the distance, and I was about to put my binoculars away when I heard a sharp whistling sound from nearby. I swung the binoculars in its direction and picked up a dumpy little bird skittering along the water's edge. The black ring round the neck and short orange bill and legs told me it was a ringed plover, a small wader. This was becoming a good day for birdwatching. I was glad again that I'd brought my little binoculars. They're not something many long-distance walkers carry but I wouldn't be without them for days like this. Birds are one of the delights of wild places.

The Watershed runs north along the boggy moorland hills east of the River Pattack. The skies were grey and the clouds moving fast. It didn't look appealing up there. I knew the walk beside the river to the Falls of Pattack was pleasant and on a good track, so I decided to stay low and look up at the Watershed rather than walk along it. I was enjoying the birds too and hoping to see more along the river, which is bordered by big flat meadows and clumps of trees, a gentle landscape contrasting with the moors above.

This really was a day for birds and enjoying the creatures of the wilds rather than the landscape. The walk along the river was a delight, the dull skies and flat light forgotten as I watched lapwings wheeling over the meadows and listened to their plaintive cries. Curlews were soaring into the sky and calling too, their bubbling song redolent of wild nature. I spotted them standing in the grass, long legs, big brown bodies and those distinctive curved bills. Even noisier were oystercatchers, their piercing cries drowning out everything else. I heard a snipe drumming and saw several zigzag through the air, wings beating fast, long bills outstretched.

The walk had slowed as I kept stopping to watch the birds. It seemed wrong to hurry. I've never viewed long-distance walks as speed marathons, never tried to do high mileages every day. Being able to enjoy where I am walking has always been important. I want the time to experience what nature has to offer. Here it was the birdlife.

Of all the birds of the day two especially pleased me. The beautiful black-throated divers because I'd never seen a family of them like this before and they are one of my favourites and, even more, the lapwings, because they brought back my childhood long ago in Formby on the Lancashire coast when I used to walk to primary school through cow pastures where lapwings wheeled and called. In my memory it was always warm and sunny. Those days when it must have rained have gone from my mind.

Leaving the meadows, the track entered woods, mostly conifer plantation but with some mixed deciduous trees beside the river, and started to descend. No longer meandering gently the river picked up speed, rushing through the trees and tumbling over the Linn of Pattack and the Falls of Pattack. The water that had been calming now invigorated me, and I too gained speed to soon reach the A86, the main road from Fort William and Spean Bridge to Strathspey. The Watershed was just brushing the western edge of the Cairngorms National Park, though still far from the Cairngorms themselves. It's a very big park, by far the largest in the UK. Turn north-east along the A86 and in around 50 miles I'd be home and still in the national park. This journey would soon turn west though.

The Watershed has been altered by humanity here. A concrete channel takes water from the River Mashie on the east side to the River Pattack and the Loch Laggan reservoir on the west, and so across the Watershed. This channel can't be crossed, it's too steep-sided and the water too fast and deep. I stayed to the west, crossing the now substantial river on a bridge.

Further human disturbance to the landscape came into view as I crossed the A86. Above the road the Watershed goes over a little hill with a pool called the Loch na Lairige near the summit. I'd thought I'd camp near the loch, but I'd reckoned without the Beauly-Denny power line, which runs across this hill. It was still being constructed at the time and the whole west and south sides of the hill were a mess of tracks, machinery, half-erected pylons and other debris. Not wanting to fight through that lot, I turned away. I didn't want to see it at all. Just a few years earlier I'd been involved in the campaign against this long line of giant pylons, representing the Mountaineering Council of Scotland on the Beauly-Denny Landscape Group, a coalition of conservation and outdoor organisations. There'd been a public inquiry. Our solicitor, working for expenses only, faced highly-paid QCs who grilled our witnesses as if they were criminals. We lost. The power line was being built.

Turning away from the devastation I re-joined the Watershed as it started on its journey back to the west, near the head of Glen Shirra. I pitched my tarp on firm turf amidst fresh, unfurling bracken fronds. The sky cleared during the evening and there was a touch of pink on the last high clouds. However, I woke to drizzle and midges. 'A rather dismal-looking day', I wrote in my journal. By the time I set off it was raining heavily, and the hills had vanished into the clouds. They stayed that way all day. High up I navigated through the mist with compass and GPS often in use. The Watershed ran along the long ridge that marks the northern boundary of the Creag Meagaidh National Nature Reserve. I'd hoped to look down into the regenerating woods in Coire Ardair, a great forest restoration success achieved simply by reducing deer numbers, but instead I just peered through dense mist to the next boulder or tussock and hunched down against the strong cold NW wind.

This ridge was significant for the walk, whether I could see anything or not, as the halfway point of the Watershed is up there, on the summit of Carn Liath. As I reached the top a figure loomed up, the first other walker I'd seen for over three days. Carn Liath is a Munro so I wasn't surprised to meet someone. A few yards into the mist and they were gone, and I was alone again. I was to see no-one else until the next evening.

I thought about being halfway and how empty the hills were as I plodded on in the cloud. Beyond Carn Liath I needed to navigate carefully as the Watershed takes an abrupt turn northwards off the ridge for a long descent to a vast bog and the slight rise between the Rivers Roy and Spey. I think I left the ridge at about the right point. At least the terrain was as expected when I finally dropped below the mist. Back up onto more shrouded hills I found a good grassy campsite beside a burn called the Allt Dubh. The day was mostly forgettable – 'a functional day', I wrote in my journal – but again there had been birds to brighten my mood: sandpipers beside the burns, snipe in the bogs, white-rumped wheatears in the heather.

I was running out of food, having supplied in Crianlarich a week before, and even though I'd eaten meals in Tyndrum, Glencoe Mountain, the Kingshouse, and the Rannoch Moor

Hotel, I could still have done with more. My appetite had soared, as it always does on long walks. Still, this next day I should reach the Great Glen and find places to eat and buy supplies. Surveying my last food didn't take long. I had just two bars left. I selected one for breakfast – a Blackfriars Apple & Sultana Flapjack – and one, a Clif Blueberry Crisp – for lunch. Combined Calories 682. I'd be hungry by evening!

From here the Watershed ran over a series of rounded moorland hills before dropping steeply to the Great Glen. Again, I was mostly walking in rain and cloud, though it was warmer as the wind was now from the south-west. The terrain was quite boggy, oozing water from all the rain and, again, I tried to stick to the Watershed but wasn't certain I'd done so. I may have crossed the highest of these hills, Carn Dearg, at least I found a cairn in about the right spot, and I certainly reached the last of them, Bheinn Bhan, from where I descended through more bogs – how could steep slopes hold so much water? – to a dense conifer plantation through which I pushed to a final top, Creag nan Gobhar, which was just in the cloud at 497 metres. This hill overlooks the Great Glen, not that I could see anything. The descent into the glen was on very steep, often tricky, terrain. I slithered and skidded through head-high bracken and dense trees and over slippery wet grass. With relief I reached the floor of the Great Glen, the A82 road and the Caledonian Canal. At just 35 metres above sea level I was at the lowest point of the Watershed.

Knowing I had mail waiting for me at the Post Office in Invergarry, which I was keen to pick up as I hadn't heard from home in a week, I decided to head that way along the Great Glen Way, hoping I could get there before the Post Office closed. I couldn't. It had been shut for an hour. I turned away, disappointed, and looked for somewhere to stay.

Before the walk I'd been invited to stay at the independent Great Glen Hostel. That lay some 5 km back down the glen. I didn't want to walk there and back again for my post the next day, so I checked into the nearby Invergarry Hotel. It was expensive, but I did have a good and very welcome dinner.

I'd planned a day off here as there was a long section coming up. However, I hadn't planned well enough. I'd thought I could resupply here but found the only shop, The Well of the Seven Heads – Lochside Larder, was more a café than a store and had little suitable for backpacking. At the Post Office I was delighted to find a package from home containing muesli, dried fruit and various bars, but it was nowhere near enough to get me through the next week or more's walking. I was lucky to get my mail too as it was a Saturday and the Post Office was closed. I just happened to turn up as the post mistress was there collecting stuff for the Royal Mail and she kindly opened for me. With few supply points in the weeks ahead I really needed to plan better. As it was, on this occasion I availed myself of the bus service to Fort Augustus and its myriad stores. This was the biggest place since Cumbernauld and, although much smaller, it was rather overwhelming. Crowds of visitors wandered the streets. I hurriedly purchased my supplies and caught the next bus back to Invergarry.

In the hotel I spent a few hours planning the rest of the walk, including researching bus and train times in case I needed to travel to resupply again, plus the opening times of Post Offices. A good Internet connection meant this was quite easy. Outside, the rain poured on.

The Great Glen is the third major geological fault line on the Watershed after the Southern Upland Fault and the Highland Boundary Fault. Running north-eastwards from coast to coast it splits the Highlands in two. The fault dates from around 430–390 million years ago. The landscape today was carved much more recently though, by glaciers in the Ice Ages some 10,000 years ago. Much of the Great Glen is filled with lochs whose floors are actually below sea level. Biggest and most famous of these is Loch Ness, supposed home of the eponymous monster.

The Great Glen marked an important stage in my walk. Beyond it was the wildest and most remote country on the Watershed and also, arguably, the most spectacular. I was looking forward to it.

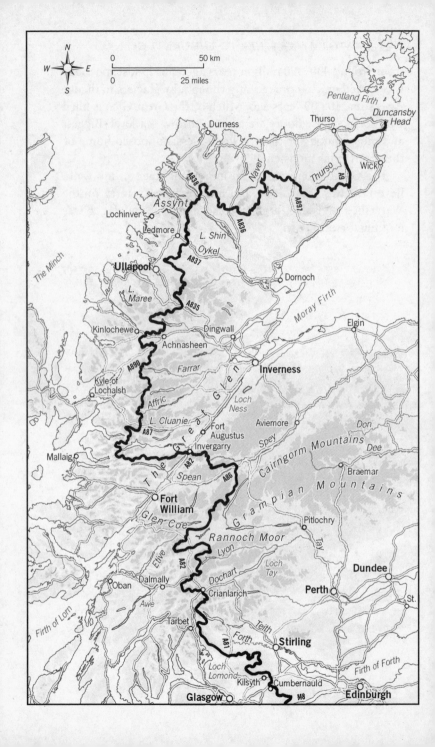

5

RAIN & SUNSHINE, DEER & BROCKEN SPECTRES

From the Great Glen the Watershed runs west for some 45 km all the way to Sgurr na Ciche in Knoydart before turning northwards again. This is rough, challenging terrain, much of which I knew well. In stormy weather it could be unpleasant and difficult. I was thinking of that as I walked back down the glen in heavy rain and strong winds to the Great Glen Hostel. If the wind was this powerful here, only a little above sea level, what would it be like on the hills?

I dripped into the hostel, my waterproofs as wet as they'd been at any time on the walk. Inside, I was damp with perspiration and condensation. I was glad to be indoors. The warden, Kirsty, was welcoming and helpful. Over lunch I discussed my plans and considered the weather. The forecast was awful – torrential rain and storm-force winds. Kirsty told me that the previous summer Colin Lock, who was running the Watershed, had called in. The forecast being similar he'd taken a lower route, paralleling the Watershed on forest tracks. This seemed a wise approach.

A saying much over-used in outdoors writing and marketing goes: 'there's no such thing as bad weather, only unsuitable clothing', or words to that effect. There are several variants. The saying is attributed to various people, including the famous Lake District guidebook writer Alfred Wainwright, polar explorer Ranulph Fiennes and comedian Billy Connolly, and also said to be a Scottish or Scandinavian proverb (with both Norway and Sweden claiming to have thought of it first). Whoever came up with it doesn't matter. It's rubbish. The suggestion that with the right clothing you can deal with any weather is laughable. No clothing will keep you on your feet in winds strong enough to blow you over, or stop you getting exhausted trying to walk. In prolonged heavy rain you'll get damp even in the best clothing. I knew this. I had the best clothing. No clothing could make navigation in dense mist easier either, or less tedious after hours of seeing nothing. This saying really needs to be relegated to the wastepaper basket.

Looking out at the wind and rain I decided to follow Colin Lock's example and head through the woods along Loch Garry to the north of the Watershed. In the trees I'd have some protection from the weather. I might see something too.

The woods proved more interesting than I expected. I'd feared the day might be spent in endless conifer plantations. Thirty years earlier that would have been the case as from the 1920s to the late 1970s the Forestry Commission planted the area with straight lines of closely packed Sitka spruce, lodgepole pine and other conifers, and felled many of the remaining Scots pines that had previously dominated the woodland here. Then a complete reversal of this policy took place and in 1985 the Commission began removing the non-native conifers and trying to undo the damage of the previous sixty years. In 1990 a large area was designated a Caledonian Forest Reserve.

Today, the Forestry Commission works with the charity Trees for Life to continue the restoration of the forest. Clifton Bain in his excellent book *The Ancient Pinewoods of Scotland* says, 'Glen Garry is an ambitious, large-scale restoration project and the beginning of an exciting revival for this ancient pinewood' and that the site is 'in transition from the devastation of the past'. The forest will never be the same, of course. The past cannot be recreated. A more natural woodland with greater biodiversity is coming about though, and I find this heartening.

I was to see much of this restoration and regeneration as I walked through the wood. Compared with most of the other forests I'd been through on the walk there was much more variety with many deciduous trees and a lack of the dark monotony of regimented plantations. At one point I followed a nature trail, at another I passed a herd of Highland cattle. Signs headed 'The Beasts are Back' and 'Hairy coos in the forest' said they were here to help create a varied habitat, replicating the effect of their ancestors that roamed wild in the ancient forest. Clifton Bain says they were introduced to graze the birch trees that have become very prolific and provide more open ground where pines can grow.

The burns flowing from the Watershed were in spate, full of dark peaty water and frothing white where they surged over rocks. There were bridges over the bigger ones. One was brand new and taped off with a sign saying 'Walk Closed. No Public Access' and pointing to a diversion. I took this as it was going in the right direction. Another very old rickety bridge was blocked with a red plastic barrier on which a sign said, 'No authorised persons allowed beyond this point'. I looked at the deep water rushing under the bridge. I wasn't going to try to ford that anywhere. I climbed the barrier and quickly crossed the bridge. It wasn't long, and I was soon across. The bridge had felt secure, but it sagged in places and the timbers did look rotten.

The heavy rain and strong winds continued, buffeting me whenever I crossed open areas between the trees. At the west end of Loch Garry I came to some ruins. Kirsty had told me that one of the buildings was still habitable and could be a shelter from the storm. I explored and found a farmhouse with rooms that were obviously used. A visitor's book said it was private and for friends and family only, but there were no notices outside nor any locks or gates. I didn't find the place very appealing anyway due to the state of the ruined buildings and the amount of detritus lying around so I moved on, intending to camp at the first suitable spot. Finding one proved rather difficult, however, as the terrain quickly became very boggy. Eventually I found a not too wet and not too bumpy spot on some open grassy ground outside of the forest. It was midnight and I'd walked 29 km. I was tired but knew that if I went to sleep without eating I'd wake in the night feeling hungry, so I had a quick supper of a bowl of Super Noodles – always a good choice for speed as they cook so fast – and a mug of hot chocolate.

I woke to the rain still hammering down and a doorway full of midges. A mosquito coil soon cleared them away. Tormentil, wild thyme and cotton grass were growing in the porch. Looking out I could see patches of blue sky and shafts of sunshine. The forecast had said this would be the best day of the week with heavy rain and even stronger winds following the day after and staying for many more days. Perhaps, I thought, I'd re-join the Watershed.

Leaving Glen Garry I followed forest roads through much less interesting conifer plantations in lower Glen Kingie. The cloud was low and there were frequent showers. Bored by the conifer monotony, I pulled out my e-reader and read my way along – *Caleb's List* by Kellan MacInnes, about the hills visible from Arthur's Seat in Edinburgh. Reading while walking, especially on roads, was nothing new. I'd done it many times before. I have a photograph taken in the Mohave Desert on the Pacific Crest Trail in 1982 of me walking along a dirt road reading a natural history guide to the Sierra Nevada. Until e-readers came along I couldn't read in the rain though. Now with one in a transparent waterproof case I could.

Whenever it came into view, the River Kingie was an impressive rain-swollen torrent. There was no sign of the drought that had preceded me. In Crianlarich and in the Great Glen Hostel I'd been told how dry it had been before I arrived. I seemed to be the rainbringer. My family had often teased me that I must be an unknowing rain god like the lorry driver in Douglas Adam's *So Long And Thanks For All The Fish*, due to the number of times the weather changed to rain on days I'd planned to go for a walk. In the book, Rob Mckenna keeps a log that shows it has rained on him every day wherever he has been. My journal was beginning to look similar.

I thought back to previous walks. There did seem to be an undue number of times it was wetter than normal. On a walk the length of the Scandinavian Mountains I was told several times it was a shame I'd picked such a wet summer for the walk – 'it's not normally like this'. On the Pacific Northwest Trail in the USA it rained most of September, which was one of the wettest on record.

Sometimes rain is a blessing though. On the Continental Divide Trail, that other watershed walk, I'd walked into a huge forest fire and had been found and escorted to safety by a trail crew who drove through the fire with trees blazing and bursting into flame all around. Rain was not forecast and it looked as though I might have to wait a while before I could walk back to where I'd been picked up. Then my cousin came to join me. It started to rain. We decided having two Brits there was the cause. The fire went out and I completed that section of the walk.

When I flew to Phoenix to start the Arizona Trail my concern was a lack of water. The winter had been very dry, and I'd been advised that the few water sources might be dry and I should cache water along the route. The plane landed in a cloud of spray. It was raining heavily. In the taxi to Flagstaff, my base for the final preparations, the driver said it never rained like this here. The next day I walked round town in my waterproofs while rain hammered down and poured off the flat roofs, which didn't have gutters as there was no need for them. There were no problems with water on the walk.

On a walk from Yosemite Valley to Death Valley in California I was concerned about how hot it would be crossing the desert. It was cloudy and cool, however, with rain threatening. After the walk was over I hitch-hiked from Death Valley to Las Vegas. The rain started just as I got a lift. It poured the whole way and then all night and the next day. I walked round Las Vegas in my waterproof jacket, which I'd never worn on the walk itself. Waiting for a taxi to the airport I talked to the doorman of the hotel. He was standing in the rain, relishing the cool water.

'This is so rare', he said.

I needed to remember these positive times. Rain wasn't always something to be complained about.

Today the predicted better weather that I'd seen hints of earlier in the day never materialised. It stayed wet and windy with low cloud on the tops. Leaving the trees, I sloshed up the bare boggy upper glen. A muddy path came and went. Across the river I could see Kinbreak bothy, its rather too bright pinky-red roof standing out startlingly against the dull brown shades of the landscape. I remembered wading across the river many years before on a similarly wet day and being disappointed when I went inside to find a sodden mud floor and no sign of use and then being elated when I spotted the ladder and found the trapdoor and the wood-lined upstairs room. Today I was passing by despite the temptation of shelter in a dry building. I hadn't walked far enough to stop yet – though if I'd really felt like it I probably would have done.

From Glen Kingie an intricate, well-designed and well-built stalker's path led up to the col between the two minor peaks of An Eag and Sgurr Beag. I had to make a decision here. An Eag was on the Watershed and just a kilometre away. From this top the Watershed ran along a dramatic rocky ridge over three Munros. On the final one, Sgurr na Ciche, it was less than 4 km from the sea at Loch Nevis yet water running east from it crossed the country to the east coast. For almost the next 20 km from An Eag the Watershed was actually west of the arm of the Atlantic called Loch Hourn.

Wind and rain swept over the col. Dark clouds made the mountains grim and foreboding. The An Eag–Sgurr na Ciche ridge is exposed. Struggling along it into this storm would be difficult and unpleasant. I'd done it in rain and wind once before, and also scared myself and a companion on one TGO Challenge when it had been covered in snow and ice. We had no ice axes or crampons and were very relieved to get down safely. Lesson learnt we then stayed low until we reached Fort William where we could acquire ice axes.

On this occasion I decided descent was the best course and dropped down a boggy path to the huge reservoir of Loch Quoich, part of the Glen Garry hydro-electric system. This massive scheme was created in 1955 when what was then the largest earth dam of its kind was built, raising the loch by 3 metres and increasing its area from 8 to 18 square km. Glenquoich Lodge, built in 1838, disappeared under the waters along with the remains of settlements cleared in the 1780s.

Today many paths and tracks run down to the water and vanish into its depths, including the one I followed down from the col. I camped close to the shore on wet ground dotted with cotton grass – but then everywhere was wet. The rain continued.

And continued. All night and all the next day. The mountains hidden in dark clouds and a fierce south-west wind sweeping the grey land, I stayed low only touching the Watershed at the dam at the west end of Loch Quoich. Everything spoke of a miserable day. But it wasn't. 'Surprisingly, much of interest', I wrote in my journal that evening. I've mentioned before how much wildlife plays in a part in my enjoyment of wild places and, on this day, I saw three birds that I hadn't seen before on this walk. The first were stonechats, bobbing and flicking their wings on the gorse bushes beside the loch. These robin-sized little birds are quite striking, especially the males with their black heads, white necks, and orange-red breasts. I usually heard them before I saw them, the distinctive call that gives them their name, like two stones being knocked together, cutting through the steady rush of the wind and rain. Then in Easter Glen Quoich I saw another handsome bird, a ring ouzel. These black thrushes with their white curved chest stripes are only found in rough wild places and are a sign of the nature of the place.

I loved seeing both the stonechats and ring ouzels, but they were forgotten when I crossed a ridge above Glen Loyne and a huge bird came gliding out of the cloud and away down the glen. A golden eagle! Magnificent! If any bird is a symbol of the wild in Scotland it's this. I've seen them many times over the years and always felt thrilled. Just this sighting alone would have kept me cheerful for many hours. Eagles can do that. I thought of another walk in a different place and very different circumstances when one had changed my mood completely. I was climbing a hot dusty ridge in the Four Peaks Wilderness on the Arizona Trail and I was hot, thirsty and fed up, the path having been washed out by a flash flood and then further destroyed by a forest fire that had burnt the whole mountainside, leaving blackened stumps and no shelter from the blazing sun. Spiky bushes, the first new growth after the fire, tore at my legs which were soon running with blood. I had little water left and two possible sources on the climb were dry. My camp that night was not enjoyable. Next day the ascent was even tougher, and I reached the top of the ridge in an unbelievably foul mood. A rush of wings swept it away as a bald eagle flew past just 50 feet away, its white head shining in the sunlight. I was entranced and suddenly the world was wonderful again. On this wet day, in weather as far from the Arizona heat as could be imagined another eagle had the same effect.

Beside the loch there were many deer, down to escape the storm like me, I guessed. They were less nervous and wary than usual. In the cold and wet they didn't want to expend any more energy than was necessary. One big stag, its massive antlers in velvet, stopped grazing to watch me pass but didn't even move when I stopped to take pictures, even though I was less than 50 metres away.

After crossing the dam, I followed the north shore of Loch Quoich for half its length. Mostly I walked on the beach – the strip of stony ground between the waterline and the high point it sometimes reached. The water level rises and falls according to the demand for electricity and the rainfall. The pale rim this leaves can look ugly and unnatural from a distance, but I found it interesting to walk along due to the amazing variety of pebbles and rocks, with masses of shapes, textures and colours. Smooth rocks, rough rocks, disintegrating rocks, striped rocks. A kaleidoscope of stone.

The beach was wide in part because of all the dry weather of a few weeks earlier. Just how dry I realised when I reached the arm of the loch that stretches up Glen Quoich. Instead of water this was a mass of mud flats and squelchy grass and I had the strange experience of being able to walk on the loch bed. All around, the hillsides were gushing with water, white torrents pouring down every faint runnel. Loch Quoich would soon fill up again.

Invigorated by the golden eagle, I finished the day by descending to camp beside the Allt Giubhais on a just big enough patch of long grass, surrounded by bogs dotted with pink-purple orchids. The name means stream of the pine wood but there wasn't a tree in sight. The rain poured on and I spent the evening in the tent. The air pressure had fallen. The storm wasn't over yet.

I woke to confusing weather signals. A touch of sunshine lit and warmed the Trailstar. At the same time, I could hear light rain pattering on the nylon and the walls were shaking in the wind. That was to be the pattern for the day – a few very short bursts of sunshine, occasional showers, and a strong wind. The sky was overcast with clouds mostly hiding the summits.

Not far from camp I came on a Cluanie Estate sign saying red deer hinds were calving and requesting people to keep to paths and ridges and out of the corries . . . 'for Your Safety and the Welfare of the Deer'. Another sign that goes against the access legislation, I thought. No dates, no times, no specific corries, and a veiled threat. Three day-walkers came up the path, the first people I'd met since leaving the Great Glen.

A track led down to Loch Cluanie, another reservoir, and the Cluanie Inn where I took refuge from the weather and had a long lunch. Situated at the head of Glen Shiel and a long way from any other hostelry or facilities, the Cluanie Inn has been a haven for walkers and climbers for well over a hundred years. I'd been here several times including one memorable occasion on my Munros and Tops walk when I arrived after completing the long South Glen Shiel Ridge (with its seven Munros) in steady rain along with Chris Brasher of Olympic gold medal, London Marathon and superb walking boots fame (I wore them on that walk), and Bill Wallace, former President of the Scottish Mountaineering Club, Trustee of the John Muir Trust, and contributor to many SMC guidebooks. Dripping wet and chilly after a long day we'd reached the inn late and found that not only was there no accommodation available but also no food – that stopped at 8 p.m. Once Bill had retrieved his car from Shiel Bridge (by asking people in the car park for a ride – the first one said he couldn't take the risk) we did a tour of the area to find every hotel or B&B for miles full and nowhere serving food. Eventually we found fish and chips in a pub in Dornie before returning to Shiel Bridge to pitch our tents on the campsite. I thought of my two companions, who had both since died, as I sat in the inn watching the rain.

The Watershed lies just a few km west of the Cluanie Inn and is probably the reason for the phenomenon called the Cluanie Curtain, which I'd first read about in the book that had inspired my long Munro walks, Hamish Brown's *Hamish's Mountain Walk*, where it's described as 'the grey sweeping rain more often met with as one nears the region'. Coming off the ocean on south-westerly winds the rain breaks over the high line of the Watershed and then, sometimes, fades away to the east. I'd seen the Curtain several times driving from the east, a grey wall rising out of Glen Shiel. I didn't see it this time. I was in it.

The wind and rain continuing, I stayed west of the Watershed when I left the inn. A walker came down the track. I said hello and received a brief gruff 'hi' in return. He didn't seem very happy. Maybe it was the weather. I saw no-one else all day. The clouds did rise at times during the afternoon, revealing Beinn Fhada looking like a spire from this side – it's actually a long mountain, which is what the name means, and then jagged and rugged Sgurr nan Ceathreamhan, hill of the quarters. Both these Munros lie on the Watershed. If the weather calmed I was hoping to climb Ceathreamhan the next day.

I re-joined the Watershed at Loch a'Bhealaich, set between the two Munros in a spectacular wild and beautiful spot. Peter Wright says camping by the loch is a special experience and it certainly was for me, though not in the way I think he meant. 'Drifting off to sleep . . . is soporific; Nature's own sleeping draught', he writes. My journal: 'a wild night and a wild morning. Torrential rain. Very strong gusty winds. Stormiest night yet. Gusts really shaking the tent'. I went out once in the wet darkness to lower the profile of the Trailstar to resist the wind better. Then I was woken again by spray hitting me in the face as rain was blown into the open entrance. For the first time on the trip I hung a piece of fabric in the doorway to keep the rain out. As an extra precaution I also slid into my waterproof bivi bag, carried in case of emergency, to keep my down sleeping bag dry.

At dawn, thick dark clouds raced overhead and the rain was arriving in dense sheets that blurred the landscape. I would not be climbing Ceathreamhan. I stared out at the storm. Going out wasn't appealing, but staying in my shaking shelter wasn't very restful or attractive either. I contemplated my sodden socks and shoes. I was at least dry in here. Well, dry enough anyway. After days and nights of rain everything starts to get a little damp. My sleeping bag was still dry enough to keep me warm though and I had dry socks to don each evening. The last I find essential. At the end of each day my wet feet were soft and wrinkled. By dawn the skin had smoothed out again, ready for another day's soaking. My mostly mesh trail running shoes didn't keep water out for more than a few seconds. I knew anyway that in prolonged wet weather nothing would keep my feet dry. The only options that would keep out the rain and the water from stream fords and deep bogs were knee-high rubber boots, and in those my feet would have been soaked in sweat and unbearably hot. Walking boots with waterproof linings can keep your feet dry for many hours, perhaps a whole day, but, in my experience, on long trips water always gets in at the top eventually and then you have boots that take a very long time to dry. At least my shoes dried fast when the rain stopped. That didn't make donning them when wet any more pleasant though.

Eventually I persuaded myself outside to find, as usual, that it wasn't quite as awful as I'd thought. The wild storm was part of what makes this land so wonderful, I told myself. On a wall at home I have a poster with a quote from John Muir 'when I heard the storm and looked out I made haste to join it; for many of Nature's finest lessons are to be found in her storms'. I felt that I was receiving rather too many of those lessons. I also felt that, like Muir, I should try and keep a positive frame of mind and seek out the rewards of whatever the weather brought. Previous experience had taught me that keeping going in wet weather was more of a mental than physical problem. Except in strong winds, walking was no more strenuous when it was raining. The challenge was keeping the mind active and engaged and not retreating into a closed unresponsive state that could lead to boredom and negative feelings. I wasn't going to abandon the walk, the weather would change at some point. So, I needed to see what the storm could show me. Two days before it had been the birds, the deer, and the stones on the loch shore. What would today bring?

Water. It brought water. Water rushing down mountain-sides in white torrents, twisting down gullies and tearing through hollows. Water underfoot, the ground like a giant sponge exuding it at every step. Water in burns I waded across, shin to knee-deep. Water flying horizontally across the land in great sheets of rain. Water in magnificent cascades on the Allt Coire Easaich – the stream of the corrie of the waterfalls.

With the Watershed now running along the cloud-hidden hills to the east I crossed boggy terrain and descended to Glen Elchaig and the remote house called Carnach where a large herd of shaggy Highland cattle with several calves were sheltering by some trees. They started moving nervously and skittering about as I approached. By the house I found a lamb tangled in a fence, its back leg trapped in the wire. I freed it quickly then decided it was time to move on as a big bull was approaching – coming to see what was disturbing his cows, I supposed. Just above the house two stags with antlers in velvet moved away slowly, reluctant to give up the little shelter they had.

I was on a wide track that led to the buildings known as Iron Lodge. I passed three small fenced woods – Scots pine, birch, rowan, and also sycamore and copper beech. Touches of forest in this bleak boggy landscape. Other people were about though I didn't see anyone. Two bicycles were propped against the fence round one wood and two tents beside Iron Lodge, a white-washed, slate-roofed house identical to Carnach. Peter Wright describes Iron Lodge as a '1980s bungalow' and an 'incongruity'. I've seen much worse. I wondered where the name came from. Presumably this was not the original Iron Lodge.

The rain and wind hadn't let up all day. To the north lay a remote bothy I'd used before in bad weather. I decided to head there for the night. Crossing a pass, the highest point of the day's walk at 465 metres, the wind almost blew me over. I pulled out my anemometer. It was gusting to 40mph. That's the speed at which walking can be dangerous. I was very glad I wasn't on the summits.

I must admit I was relieved when the white-washed walls of Maol Bhuidhe came into view. In the main room I found a young Australian woman with her wet gear strewn everywhere. She was heading for Shiel Bridge having started further north at Strathcarron. Having camped the previous night like me she'd headed for the bothy for somewhere to dry out. Leaving her to the big room I moved into a tiny one next door. The floor, walls and ceiling were wood-panelled and there was a deep windowsill where I set up my kitchen. Another walker arrived much later and went upstairs, where there was another large room.

This was the first bothy I'd used during the walk and I was looking forward to a night somewhere that didn't shake in the wind and where I had a bit more room. Not that the Trailstar had let me down but after four wet and windy nights it did feel good to be indoors. I didn't have much wet gear other than my shoes and socks either as my waterproofs had kept me dry and my pack had kept out the rain. Having good gear makes a big difference in prolonged stormy weather.

Bothies are abandoned buildings once used by shepherds, gamekeepers or other estate workers. Often built in the nineteenth century they fell into disuse in the twentieth when changes in transport and land use made having workers resident in such remote places unnecessary. Mountaineers and hillwalkers soon discovered that these old buildings could provide shelter and began to use them. However,

111

occasional makeshift repairs weren't enough to stop the buildings deteriorating and most might well have become ruins but for the foresight of a group of outdoors people in 1965 who set up the Mountain Bothies Association with the aim of maintaining these simple shelters. The MBA has flourished since and looks after a network of around one hundred bothies, with the owners' blessings – the MBA doesn't own the bothies. Most are in Scotland but there are some in England and Wales.

Bothies provide four walls and a roof and not much more. Some have wooden sleeping platforms, some have fireplaces, though you'll probably have to carry in fuel to use them. They're basically a solid substitute for a tent. All your other camping gear – sleeping bag, sleeping mat, stove and cooking stuff, warm clothing – is still needed. This can sometimes catch people out, especially ones from overseas who think they'll offer the same facilities as an alpine hut. I've met quite a few disappointed walkers over the years who were expecting to find food supplies, cooking stoves, beds and more. In the last decades of the twentieth century it was hard to find much information about bothies. Now that information is easily available via the Internet (the MBA has an excellent website) and there's even a glossy guidebook.

It was in England that I discovered bothies, on my first real backpacking trip, the Pennine Way in 1976. As a student I chose to do the walk in April during the Easter vacation. The weather was rather like that I was experiencing now, on the Watershed, only colder and with snow rather than rain at times. On the highest section of the route from Knock Fell to Cross Fell I met two day-walkers heading the other way in the mist. They told me there was a bothy just beyond Cross Fell. My guidebook, A. Wainwright's *Pennine Way Companion*, mentioned an old mine cottage that would make 'a good shelter and bivouac in emergency' and there was somewhere called Greg's Hut marked on my Ordnance Survey map. It wasn't an emergency but when I found it in the dense mist that had descended I decided to stay, 'never having slept in a bothy before', as I wrote in my journal. The little one-roomed hut, which was indeed an old mine building, had been renovated by the MBA not many years before in memory of a mountaineer called John Gregory who'd been killed skiing in the Alps. I had that first bothy night to myself. There was coal and wood, so I lit a fire to dry out my wet gear and spent the evening reading old MBA journals by the light of a Tilley lamp. I'd never heard of the organisation before.

I was glad I'd stayed when I woke to strong winds battering the bothy, and the clouds still low on the hills. 'This place is a really good idea – I hope people respect it. It could be a real lifesaver', I wrote over breakfast. 'I must send the MBA some money when I get home'. What I actually did was join and I've been a member ever since, though an inactive one as I've never made it to a work party. Over the years I've stayed in many bothies, often to escape stormy weather. If it's fine I do prefer to camp but I always like to know where the nearest bothies are in case the weather changes. I was certainly glad I knew of this one.

Maol Bhuidhe is one of the remotest bothies. It's first mentioned in the National Census of 1841 when it was inhabited by gamekeeper Donald MacRae, his wife and two servants. Living here then it would have felt far more cut off than it does now. Over the next seventy years a succession of keepers and shepherds and their families lived here. The building was abandoned in 1916, and when the MBA took it over in the late 1960s it was in poor repair. Since then though it has been a weathertight shelter.

The Australian walker was off early. I lingered in the hope of an improvement in the weather. I really wanted to re-join the Watershed, which lay some 3 km away and went over the hill that rose directly above the bothy, Beinn Dronaig. As I was making another mug of coffee the walker from upstairs appeared. He was in no hurry either and we talked away the morning. Jonathan described himself as an artist and environmentalist from Yorkshire. He was five days into a seven-week stravaig and the word, which means to wander about with no aim or destination, was appropriate as he had no set route and his only maps were from a road atlas. He'd started in Inverness and was heading west and maybe going to the Isle of Lewis from Ullapool to visit the Callanish stone circle and then returning to the mainland and following the coast round to Wick. His gear was old and battered, looking like the stuff I'd used on the Pennine Way rather than the stuff I used now. If I hadn't spent much of the last few decades reviewing equipment for outdoor magazines I might well still be using some of my forty-year-old gear, I reflected.

Our conversation didn't touch on gear though. Instead it ranged over walking, conservation, nature and art. I hadn't talked about such issues in any depth since I'd left Peter Wright at the start of the walk and I found the morning fascinating and stimulating. Such discussions went on with myself in my head at times while I walked, and the books I read in camp, currently Jim Crumley's excellent *The Great Wood*, prompted much thinking, but to actually talk to someone else and hear and respond to other views was a delight. Although I hadn't consciously done so I realised that conversations like this were one of the things I missed on long solo walks. Meeting people like Jonathan are one of the advantages of bothies. You never know who else might be there.

I always carry a tent even if planning on using a bothy, as sometimes a bothy might be full or the other visitors might want to party into the small hours. I've stuck my head in a few bothies over the years, peering through the steaming wet clothing hanging from the rafters at all the sleeping mats covering the floor and decided a tent in a storm isn't a bad idea after all. Sometimes I've moved after settling in when a large group has appeared. Being squeezed into a corner by a boisterous party who all know each other isn't always fun. Bothies are a Scottish phenomenon (well, British now but here is where they started) but many countries have mountain huts and even unlocked shelters. In the White Mountains of New Hampshire there are three-sided lean-to wooden shelters that function in much the same way. One autumn I made a traverse of the highest peaks in these mountains, the Presidential Range – all the summits named after US Presidents. The White Mountains are noted for severe weather and on a day of lashing rain and high winds I decided to stay in one of the lean-tos. I'd just settled in and was about to cook dinner when a school party arrived. They were friendly and apologetic, but they weren't going anywhere else. I camped in the rain and probably slept better than I would have done in a shelter full of teenagers.

Sometimes unexpectedly sharing can be wonderful though. On a solo ski tour in Norway I met a group of Norwegians heading for the same hut as me. (In Norway they are locked but if you join the organisation that runs them you can get a key.) We were in a near white-out, navigation was difficult and I ended up sharing route-finding with the leader of the group. I'd noticed that they all had huge loads, much bigger than the ones usually needed even in winter. The reason became apparent in the hut when they pulled out masses of fresh food and bottles of wine. It was an annual works outing and they always dined luxuriously. I pulled out my dehydrated rations. 'No, no', I was told, 'you're with us. Come and eat and drink. We have plenty'. They did, and I did. That was one party I didn't mind joining.

During the morning there were hints of sunshine though the wind was still strong and the tops in cloud. I didn't set off until early afternoon and by then the weather was deteriorating again. I headed straight up Beinn Dronaig intending to join the Watershed on the top. I was soon in thick mist and being blown about by a blustery wind. A circular trig point loomed up in the cloud. I sheltered from the wind for a quick bite to eat then began a difficult and hazardous descent down the steep, greasy, craggy north face of the hill. 'Like Ben Lui all over again', I wrote in my journal. There would be no more summits that day. Ben Dronaig was 797 metres high and I'd had problems staying upright in the blustery wind. The Watershed now went over five Munros, rising to 1,053 metres. Again, fighting through the wind and seeing nothing in the cloud didn't appeal so I stayed west of the Watershed and followed glens and passes before descending to Glen Carron, not far from Achnashellach. I was tempted by another bothy, Bearnais, en route but wanted to reach the glen. A main road and railway run down Glen Carron and it took me a while to find a site hidden from both by a screen of trees and dense gorse bushes. Not that I needed to hide, I just preferred being out of sight. My camp gave lovely views along the River Carron and across the glen to birch-clad craggy slopes.

It was now six days since I'd left the Great Glen and my supplies were running low. My plan had been to drop down to Kinlochewe in a day or so, which would probably require hitch-hiking. Resupplying for a Watershed walk in the northern Highlands is difficult as there are few villages and most are at sea level, and so require a long diversion. However, as I was unexpectedly close to Achnashellach Station I thought I'd see if there was a train to Strathcarron and maybe take a day off. Even with my lower route I was feeling battered by the weather, physically and psychologically. A rest appealed. So did not hitch-hiking. That was something I'd done often when a student over forty years previously but only out of necessity. I knew people who enjoyed the uncertainty, the chance meetings, the romance of 'life on the road'. I didn't. I just wanted to get where I was going and then start doing the things I wanted to do. Rushing up and down roads in strangers' vehicles, being dropped in the middle of rainy nights in the middle of nowhere, watching lines of cars speed past for hour after hour. None of that was for me. But on long walks there are times when supply points lie some distance off route and the only way to reach them is hitch-hiking or long road walks. On popular long-distance trails in the USA and other countries this is an established practice and there are 'trail angels' who look out for hikers needing lifts. In the Highlands people did sometimes hitch-hike back to their car or camp after a hill walk – I've given lifts to some over the years. If I had to hitch-hike I would, but I'd avoid if at all possible and this seemed an opportunity to do so.

A strong gusty wind shaking the tent woke me early in the morning. I was camped just 33 metres above sea level. That settled my thoughts. This was not a day for the tops. I hacked away through the trees to the road and followed it to the station. By chance I didn't have to wait long for a train and ten minutes after catching it I was embarking at Strathcarron further down the glen. A sign pointed to Lochcarron, where the shops were. Three miles. I set out walking. A car came past, stopped. 'Want a lift?' I accepted gratefully. The driver recognised me. She was from Carrbridge, not far from

Grantown-on-Spey and had seen me in cafés in the town. By lunchtime I was ensconced in the Lochcarron Bistro looking out at the rain. I would be back there for dinner.

A night indoors and the opportunity to dry my footwear wasn't to be missed so I checked into the very pleasant Pathend B&B. Here the owner recognised my name as he had my Isle of Skye guidebook and offered to take me back to Strathcarron station the next morning. This unplanned day off was turning out well. It continued to as I found the Spar shop had an excellent selection of food suitable for backpacking. Heavy rain all afternoon and evening further confirmed my decision. I was glad not to be out in this. Very glad.

Overnight the rain and wind faded away and I woke to a calm and dry day. I felt relieved. The constant stormy weather was beginning to wear me down. I then felt elated on hearing the weather forecast. This fine weather could last for ten days. I knew forecasts for that far ahead were hardly reliable, but I did think this could mean at least a few nice days. I set off feeling quite light-hearted.

This feeling was somewhat subdued by the start of the walking from Achnashellach Station. There are big conifer plantations here and much clear-cutting was going on, and the path I'd hoped to take was closed with a diversion in place. I didn't mind that, but the huge clear-cut areas were an ugly eyesore. It takes decades for the land to recover from such violence. I accept that these are commercial crops but selective felling with trees thinned out, rather than removed completely to leave a devastated landscape, would be far preferable. Masses of tall foxgloves lined the forest track, their purple flowers contrasting with bright yellow coltsfoot lightened my mood.

I was heading over the Coulin Pass, a fine way to reach Glen Torridon from Glen Carron, and then east to pick up the Watershed again on the slopes of Carn Loisgte and follow it over a series of rolling hills with superb views of Torridon giant Beinn Eighe and a mass of higher hills stretching out in every direction. Having views again was wonderful. I could see the Watershed stretching out ahead of me. For the first time in many days I felt in touch with it again. From Bidein Clann Raonaild I had a dramatic view down to Loch Maree with Beinn Eighe and Slioch rising either side. A steep descent led to the A832 and a view down long Glen Docherty. Kinlochewe lay that way. There wasn't much traffic and I was glad I wasn't hitch-hiking there.

These little-visited relatively low moorland hills (400–500 metres) were full of wildlife. There were many herds of deer, ensuring no young trees could grow. Golden plover perched on tussocks and flew low across the heather. I heard many more calling than I saw. There were dotterel too, another handsome plover with a chestnut breast and a white stripe above the eye. On a little lochan I spied four small ducks. Binoculars out I identified them as teal, a new species for the walk.

I camped on a col between two of the hills with stunning views all around, the finest camp I'd had for quite a while and it was actually on the Watershed too. There was just enough of a breeze to keep the midges away and I sat outside, relishing the freedom of not having to shelter in the Trailstar and of being able to see where I was. I sat outside for breakfast too, after a calm night. A few clegs, those large flies with a nasty bite, buzzed round me but were easily swatted away if they landed.

The day that followed was one of the best on the walk so far. 'Superb mountain views all day and much wildlife', I wrote in the evening. The latter started as I was climbing Meall a'Chaorainn early in the day. Without knowing why, I felt there was something behind me. I turned and just 50 metres away a golden eagle was gliding past not much above head height and looking at me. I watched it curve round the contour of the hill and pass out of sight. What a way to start the day!

I descended to a mass of peat hags at the head of appropriately named Coire Bog and started up Fionn Bheinn, the first Munro I'd climbed since Carn Liath on the other side of the Great Glen nine days ago. It felt longer. That part of the walk felt distant, almost a different time. That happens on long walks, I've found. The immediacy of hour to hour, day to day, can make earlier parts of the walk feel remote.

Fionn Bheinn is a big grassy lump of a hill but it does have tremendous views as it's quite a way from anything of comparable height. To the west the strange and dramatic prehistoric shapes of Torridonian sandstone mountains ranged along the skyline. To the north-west the great block of Slioch and high remote Lochan Fada, by which I'd camped many times, were particularly dominant. Further north the jagged outline of An Teallach rose into the blue sky. Turning eastwards I could see the less rugged but still splendid line of the Fannichs, of which Fionn Bheinn is an outlier. I'd soon be on those hills but first I followed the Watershed on a westward loop over more outliers.

Descending towards Loch Fannich I was startled when a big fox, really red in colour, sprang out of a peat hag only 10 metres away and then sped off downhill. Just before the loch the Watershed turns away to climb another hill after crossing a big concrete pipe carried on concrete supports. This takes water from burns on Fionn Bheinn into Loch Fannich, as part of a hydro-electric scheme. The pipeline is an ugly intrusion into the landscape but not as much as a hideous bulldozed track I could see traversing the hillside not far away.

The real damage to this land wasn't caused by pipes or tracks though, but by deer. I couldn't see a single tree anywhere. On long narrow Beinn nan Ramh (the name means the hill of the oar) I did see hundreds of deer, by far the largest number so far. I'd been thinking about deer since I'd reached the Highlands. Whilst I was walking through a wild landscape it wasn't a healthy one. The ecosystem was drastically out of balance, with poor biodiversity, and one of the main reasons for this was overgrazing by deer. There should be far more trees. How the trees disappeared is complex and to do with a mix of climate changes and felling but what isn't that complicated is that overgrazing prevents regeneration. There are, simply, far too many deer. The rise of sporting estates in the Victorian era saw a rise in deer numbers, often replacing the sheep that had previously been responsible for overgrazing. High deer numbers are not good for the land. They have no natural predators, wolves having long been exterminated, so the only control on numbers is by shooting. Sporting estates generally don't want to reduce deer numbers much, if at all – shooting them is what their business is all about and they want to ensure there are plenty so clients aren't disappointed.

There used to be an argument that the land had changed and was no longer suitable for trees, so they wouldn't return even if deer numbers were reduced. This has been disproven many times on various estates by shooting or by fencing the deer out. The first place to do this, in the 1950s, was the Beinn Eighe National Nature Reserve, where there is now a flourishing forest. More recently the same has occurred on the Creag Meagaidh National Nature Reserve. These were both places not far from the Watershed.

Red deer are magnificent animals and I never tire of seeing them, despite knowing the damage they do. Originally, they were forest animals, as they still are in much of mainland Europe but, in the Highlands, they have adapted to the open hill. I don't like the idea of shooting them and I've never understood how anyone enjoys killing them but with no natural predators it's the only way to keep numbers down. Fencing can also be effective, but this results in blocks of healthy land amongst blocks of degraded land, which looks and feels unnatural. Also, in severe winters deer come down into the glens. If they are fenced out they can die of starvation and cold, often up against the fences and within sight of shelter. This seems to me to be crueller than shooting.

I'd learnt many years before that the Highland landscape is not as it could and should be, that there was a dearth of trees and wildlife. (I first read about this in Frank Fraser Darling's important book *The Highlands and Islands* where he describes the Highlands as a 'devastated terrain' but what this meant didn't sink in until I first walked through the magnificent forests of the Sierra Nevada in California and saw what healthy forest and mountain landscapes were like.) That didn't detract from my love of the area or enjoyment of its wildness, but it did engender sadness when I walked through empty glens where there could be forests and wildlife and perhaps people too, living amongst the trees. Ironically, I was aware that the stormy weather of previous weeks that had severely curtailed what I could see and that had made the actual physical act of walking more of a challenge had meant that I hadn't registered the lack of trees anything like as much as I would have done if it had been fine. Now it was, and I was looking across these vast areas of bare land at vast herds of deer.

The return of trees would bring about a more diverse landscape suitable for a greater variety of wildlife. I thought back to the contrast between the bare Southern Upland hills and the richer landscape and wildlife of the Central Lowlands, something I really hadn't expected. The Highlands were just as degraded as the Uplands in many areas.

There's no going back to the past, of course. The forest of 250 years ago can't be recreated, let alone that of 1,000, 5,000 or 9,000 years ago. Our new forests will be what suits the land now, and they'll include new species too, including the much-maligned Sitka spruce. There's no way the tree that is by far the commonest in Scotland won't have a place in any new woods. I see no reason why it shouldn't either. What's needed is a mix of trees growing naturally rather than tightly-packed plantation crops. I've seen many self-seeded Sitka spruce that have escaped the confines of the plantations. There will be more. Larch is another introduced species that will be part of the new forests. Because larch woods are open and airy, and the trees look wonderful in spring and autumn, people generally have far less objection to them than to spruce in its dark, gloomy plantations. Free the spruces though and they become magnificent trees. I'd seen them in the distant Pacific Northwest of the USA and marvelled at their size and splendour. There, Sitka spruce can grow to almost 100 metres – the tallest in Britain is in Perthshire and reaches 61 metres. As the fifth largest and third tallest conifer it's one of the world's biggest trees as well as the largest species of spruce. We really ought to give it more respect!

Sitka spruce has a strong Scottish connection. The first seeds were planted in Britain in 1831, having been sent back by Scottish plant collector David Douglas, who made three expeditions to the Pacific Northwest between 1823 and 1832. He collected hundreds of species and is reckoned to have introduced around 240 to Britain including the Douglas fir, which is named after him. (His fascinating story is well-told in Ann Lindsay and Syd House's *The Tree Collector: The Life and Explorations of David Douglas*.) Douglas was aware of the potential value of Sitka spruce, writing: 'it possesses one great advantage by growing to a very large size . . . in apparently poor, thin damp soils . . . this unquestionably has great claims on our consideration as it would thrive in such places in Britain where *P. sylvestris* (Scots pine) finds no shelter. It would become a useful and large tree'. I suspect that he would be amazed at just how successful it has become.

Douglas wasn't the first European to identify Sitka spruce or Douglas fir. That was another Scotsman, Archibald Menzies, who was the botanist on Captain George Vancouver's expedition to the west coast of North America in the 1790s and whose name is remembered in the scientific name for the Douglas fir – *Pseudotsuga menziesii*. Menzies liked the Sitka spruce for the anti-scurvy properties of its needles. The tree is named for the town of Sitka in southern Alaska (it's the state tree).

Sitka spruce is well-suited to Scotland's damp maritime climate and grows very fast, producing good quality timber in forty or so years, hence its popularity for commercial forestry. Left alone, trees can live for 600 years. Not all Sitka plantations are viable for timber. Many were planted in areas hard to access and on boggy ground that makes the use of heavy machinery difficult or impossible. In some areas the trees don't grow well. Some forests have never been thinned or managed in any way – which can mean they are returning to a more natural condition as trees are blown down and clearings are created. These abandoned plantations still have a dearth of biodiversity and could do with different trees being introduced. This is now the aim of the Forestry Commission Scotland so hopefully these old plantations will be renewed and healthier ecologically, as will all new plantations.

Wildlife doesn't generally object to spruce or larch or other trees either. Red squirrels want conifers – they don't care what sort they are. Other creatures are the same, as long as the forest has some diversity with a mix of trees, open glades, and flourishing undergrowth. Then there are the animals that should be here but are no longer. Beavers in the rivers, lynx in the forests, eventually wolves, and also moose. These would bring more health back to the land. 'Rewild' it, to use the current in-word. Especially the predators, which alter the behaviour of other animals leading to many unforeseen but positive changes, as shown by the effects of reintroducing wolves to Yellowstone National Park in the USA.

Reintroducing missing species would also bring excitement and joy. I've walked many miles through land with wolves, bears, moose and lynx and have had the great privilege and pleasure of encounters with the first three. Just knowing they are there is a thrill and makes nature wilder and more whole. I'd love to hear wolves howling along the Watershed and know that lynx are prowling in the forests (as the latter might be before too long – David Hetherington's *The Lynx and Us* argues well why reintroducing them to the Highlands is feasible).

Feeling thirsty I discovered I'd lost my water bottle – left on the summit of Fionn Bheinn, I suspected. I wasn't going back for it! Instead, I used my mug to dip water from the many burns until I found an old plastic drinks bottle beside one. I hoped whoever found mine would find it as useful as I did this one. Having rounded the headwaters of Loch Fannich I camped on a wide expanse of boggy ground before the Watershed turned east for a long traverse of the main Fannichs summits. To the west Slioch rose into the sky, sharp and dramatic.

Dawn set the pattern for the next day. A strong breeze blew clouds across the sky, sometimes hiding the summits, sometimes parting to reveal blue sky and shafts of sunlight. The

Watershed runs along the main spine of the Fannichs over five Munros so there is much ascent and descent on this fine high-level walk. The clouds came and went. The slopes were as bare as those of the day before and I saw deer all day, sometimes herds of a hundred and more and from the glen floor to the summits. There was other wildlife too. I watched a pair of golden eagles for a while, reckoning they were nesting on a crag they landed on. Descending from Sgurr Mor, the highest Fannich peak, I put up a flock of eight ptarmigan which scuttled off low to the ground staying close together. No sound, no flight, a family hoping I hadn't noticed them, I thought.

Whilst the clouds came and went, allowing good views from the westernmost peaks, the higher eastern ones were enveloped in white when I crossed them. I did have one sudden view when the clouds ripped apart and I could look through a huge hole down to the glen below. Late in the evening the sun was a red ball in the mist as I climbed Sgurr Mor. The cloud couldn't reach far above. If the summit had been a few hundred metres higher I might have passed through it. As it was, the hazy sun was my only view.

On the summit a lightly clad runner with a small pack was sitting, and I discovered he knew Peter Wright from involvement with the Duke of Edinburgh Award. I mused on the sometimes small-seeming world of the Scottish outdoors. That the first person I'd spoken to in three days should know Peter did feel a little surprising. He was planning on bivvying on a summit I'd just crossed. Heading the other way, I descended to the col before the next Munro and decided to camp. There was water and the breeze had dropped. 'Probably spectacular if mist lifts', I wrote in my journal. It did, and it was.

I woke to a cloud inversion and sunshine. The higher peaks were sharp and clear. The top of the mist wasn't far below so

126

most of the world was flat and white. The air was calm and still, the Trailstar soaked inside and out with dew and condensation. The thin mist rose and drifted over my camp, the sun still visible as a weak pale orb. Wandering over to the edge of the steep craggy slopes that lay to the north I caught the sun again and watched as a big semi-circle of red, yellow and blue around a dark figure formed on the mist below, a Brocken Spectre. The name comes from the Brocken, a peak in Germany's Harz Mountains, where it was first described in 1780. It forms when the sun casts someone's shadow onto mist below. It's a wonderful atmospheric effect that is always thrilling to see.

Eventually the mist settled just below the level of my camp. Revelling in the sunshine and the views, I wandered round soaking it all in, reluctant to leave. It was one of the finest camps of the walk. Another atmospheric phenomenon appeared, a fog bow or white rainbow curving across the mist. It was a glorious, glorious morning.

Finally departing, I climbed the last Fannich Munro, Beinn Liath Mhòr Fannaich, with tremendous views, especially west to the ragged outline of An Teallach, a superb mountain I have been up several times but have yet to see except from afar as it's always been in cloud. Today it was clear and enticing. It's not on or near the Watershed though so I turned my eyes north to Beinn Dearg, which is, and which is also a fine hill, though without the majestic complexity of An Teallach.

First though, I had not only to descend out of the Fannichs but also find my way to sea level and Ullapool. I needed to resupply. There would be nowhere else for over a week unless I made an even longer diversion. Below me was the main road to Ullapool where I hoped to hitch a lift. I followed the Watershed down to Loch Droma and the A835. There wasn't much traffic, and none of it was interested in picking up a hot sweaty scruffy walker with a big pack. I checked my phone. I had a signal. I gave in and called a taxi. A few hours later I was wandering round Ullapool looking for somewhere to stay. Everywhere was full. I was told there was a big international rowing event taking place. Eventually I tried the big Royal Hotel, hoping if there was a room it wasn't too expensive. Success! The hotel had plenty of rooms and the cost was less than the full B&Bs I'd tried. I wondered if others had assumed it would be costly to stay here.

Ullapool shone in the sunshine. I needed a day here to prepare for the next section. I really hoped this weather would last.

6

LAST DAYS IN THE MOUNTAINS

Ullapool was hot and in summer mood. Tourists in dark glasses strolled the harbour front in shorts and T-shirts, licking ice creams, or lazed in pavement cafés over cold drinks. The sea was deep blue and the sky only a little paler. I like Ullapool and its artistic and nautical air. It feels friendly and different. I had much to do though, so couldn't spend much time simply enjoying being here. This might well be my last day off.

I hoped it wouldn't be my last supply point as well, as there was probably a fortnight's walking still to do and I didn't want to carry food for that long. I couldn't, though, remember what my plans were and hadn't written anything in my notebook. So, my first task was to collect my final packet of maps from the Post Office and return to the hotel to spread them all over the floor and do some thinking and planning, scrawling in my notebook stuff I should really have done before starting. I don't like too much advance organisation, it takes the spontaneity out of a walk. Sometimes though, I go too far the other way, and certainly felt I had now. From the maps I worked out there were only two feasible supply points ahead and the only one of them near the Watershed was ten days' walking from Ullapool, which would mean carrying rather a lot of food. The alternative would mean hitch-hiking

129

or possibly catching a train – I downloaded times – and would certainly involve a whole day away from the walk.

A compromise. I'd buy eight days' food and see how far it got me.

Ullapool had everything I needed. I treated myself to one expensive freeze-dried backpacking dinner – five times the cost of the supermarket dehydrated meals I usually ate. Eating it a few nights later reminded me why I didn't buy such meals – 'bland and not enough. Prefer Batchelor's!' I noted, the last a reference to the Pasta 'n Sauce and Super Noodles meals that made up much of my diet. Dinner in the hotel that evening was 'adequate but not exciting'. I didn't record what it was – I don't think I'll go far as a restaurant critic or food writer. I did have an excellent pint of Suilven, a golden ale from the An Teallach brewery, which wasn't far away.

Clouds rolled in overnight and I left Ullapool by taxi – I'd had it with trying to hitch-hike – under an overcast sky, and returned to Loch Droma. A warm brisk south-west wind kept the midges at bay as I set off for the Beinn Dearg range. The walking was easy on good paths and the tops were clear of the clouds, giving wide-ranging but hazy and rather flat views. The terrain grew rougher and rockier as I approached the intriguingly named Iorguill – it means 'the uproar' or 'skirmish'. Beyond the summit, flat slabs made for almost pavement-like walking to the edge of the crags rimming deep Gleann na Squaib and a lovely and strange drystane dyke (drystone wall) that ran almost all the way to the summit of Beinn Dearg. This dyke has been cleverly built from a wide assortment of angular sharp-edged rocks, mostly quartzite. I'm often impressed with stone walls, but this one amazed me. Fitting together such disparate shapes must have taken many hours of painstaking work.

The ascent of Beinn Dearg – the red mountain – along the Watershed is fairly easy, just a long walk up stony slopes. The hill presents a very different prospect on the imposing north and east sides where it's steep and craggy. Across a big drop the rocky pyramid of Cona' Mheall rises to the east. The name means 'adjoining hill', appropriately as it joins Beinn Dearg at the high Bealach a' Choire Ghranda and is separate from the main ridge, which runs northwards. Choire Ghranda itself is fine and wild and filled with a big lochan. The summit of Beinn Dearg really is a splendid spot.

Beinn Dearg and Cona' Mheall are both Munros. In fact, at 1,084 metres Beinn Dearg is the highest hill north of the Ullapool-Dingwall road. There are only six Munros further north with three of these close by and soon crossed by the Watershed. They lie on a long twisting line of high ground that runs around the head of big Gleann Beag, which you can see clearly from Beinn Dearg. Leaving the grand summit viewpoint with its wide-ranging views of hills and glens rolling into the distance I walked over the first two of these lower Munros. I could hardly say I climbed them, there's only little dips and short ascents – all the work had been done on Beinn Dearg. Meall nan Ceapraichean (hill of the stubby hillocks) and Eididh nan Clach Geala (web of the white stones) look quite impressive viewed from the glens to the west but seem just bumps on the broad upland ridge when approached this way. According to Peter Drummond in *Scottish Hill Names* the lovely name Eididh nan Clach Geala refers to 'the intricate pattern of quartzite blocks shifted into geometric shapes by frost movements'. The walking is easy and enjoyable and the views vast. I wore sandals all day.

The terrain grows more rugged as the fourth Munro is approached. Seana Bhraigh (old height) is one of the remotest Munros and has a magnificent craggy northern face stretching some 5 km. From the south it's just another rise, albeit a little steeper and higher. The glory lies below the summit where rocky slopes drop steeply into the deep bowl of Cadha Dearg. The views all around are wild and magnificent. Having camped here before, I was keen to do so again and glad the weather was calm. The top of Seana Bhraigh was in cloud and the sky overcast but there was barely a breeze and it stayed dry. I pitched the Trailstar looking down to the reed-girt pool of little Loch a' Chada-Dheirg where three small dark ducks were swimming, too far away to identify even with my binoculars. I was high in the hills and could sit outside and watch the sky darken. I relished the peace and quiet. Nothing moved and there was no sound.

On the tops I'd seen a few deer but no other wildlife. One spring trip, many years before, I'd been surprised to see a badger up here and watched it for quite a while as it explored nooks and crannies and wandered across the remaining snow banks.

Wildlife has become a controversial topic in this area, thanks to the Alladale Wilderness Reserve, which lies just to the east and includes Carn Ban, one of the remotest Corbetts, some 5 km from Sean Bhraigh. The Alladale Estate was turned into the Reserve by Paul Lister, who bought it in 2003. His highly laudable aim is to restore the area to a more natural state with a renewed forest and the reintroduction of missing animals. To promote the first, deer numbers have been reduced and hundreds of thousands of trees planted to go along with natural regeneration. Controversy arrives with the proposal to introduce wolves and bears. Unsurprisingly, this has provoked opposition from neighbouring estates, farmers and others for whom the mention of these big predators sets alarm bells ringing. For completely different reasons it's also outraged walkers and climbers' organisations along with some conservationists because Lister proposes building a huge fence round the estate to keep the animals in. As well as being an eyesore – it would have to be tall and it would run over summits and so stand out from afar – it would go against the access legislation. Only by paying to go on safari with guides (Lister's models are South African game reserves) would access be allowed.

Looking over this vast landscape I couldn't imagine it being sullied with a tall fence and accompanying service tracks. That would be horrible. I think the forest work being done and the overall aims for Alladale are wonderful and something I'd like to see many more estates take up. I'd also like to see missing wildlife reintroduced, but not into a fenced enclosure, a zoo in all but name however large. You can't fence in the wild. Also, for a healthy population, animals need to be able to move freely between areas and interbreed. Alladale is nowhere near big enough to sustain wolves or bears.

There has also been some concern from walkers that large predators such as these would be dangerous, and used to keep people off the hills. This is not so. Both are wary of humans (wisely) and not a threat. They exist in many mainland Europe countries and their range, especially that of wolves, is spreading. The risk of being attacked is extremely slim – domestic dogs are a far greater threat. I've never even seen a trace of wolves or bears when walking in places where they live in Europe. In Canada I have seen wolves twice and heard them howling a few times more, a sign that you really are somewhere wild. Any sighting of wolves or bears is a fantastically thrilling experience. I've seen many bears in North America too, sometimes quite close, and it's always an exciting experience. Their presence changes the behaviour of prey animals and can have a profound effect on the environment, as shown by the impact of wolves on Yellowstone National Park in the USA since their reintroduction in 1995. This is known by the lovely term 'trophic cascade'.

Whilst having wolves and bears in the Highlands is something I dream of, I can't see it happening for many years, if it ever does. There would have to be general agreement it was the right thing to do, and the animals would have to be free to roam. More realistically the lynx could be introduced in many areas now. David Hetherington, in his beautifully illustrated book *The Lynx and Us*, shows that there's enough woodland with connecting corridors for them to thrive. Beavers, which are already present in a few areas, could be introduced in many other areas too.

I wish Alladale well. I'm in total agreement with the aim of 'restoring the Highland ecosystem'. But I could never support a fence over the hills or a restriction on access. By pushing for these, Paul Lister risks alienating many who would otherwise support him.

Thinking about wildlife and rewilding I pondered the power of words. Two books I read during the walk – Jim Crumley's *The Last Wolf*, which I'd read early on in the Southern Uplands, and George Monbiot's *Feral: Searching for enchantment on the frontiers of rewilding*, which I was reading as I sat outside the Trailstar below Seana Bhraigh – gave me a great deal to consider. Certain words provoke strong reactions. 'Wolves' is one. 'Rewilding' is another. I shudder when I hear anyone refer to 'vermin' or 'pests' in reference to any creature that might eat other creatures that hunters and gamekeepers want to kill. These negative words essentially say that such creatures aren't worth anything and it's fine to slaughter them, indeed it may be a duty to do so. That way hen harriers, eagles, red kites, foxes, stoats, pine martens and more can all be dismissed. Often those saying this claim their aim is to protect wildlife. This is to divide wildlife into good wildlife and bad wildlife, rather like the deserving and undeserving poor of the nineteenth century (and a view that hasn't gone away unfortunately). Wildlife is wildlife. All wildlife. No species is more deserving than another.

The use of words by conservationists worries me too at times. Hearing grey squirrels called 'tree rats' ('rat', there's another negative word) and 'pests' again suggests killing them is fine and that, somehow, they don't deserve to exist. They may not be 'native', having been introduced in the late nineteenth century from the USA, but they've been here for many generations now, given that their average lifespan is four to six years. They are blamed for damaging forestry and causing the extinction of red squirrels, which suddenly become the 'nice' squirrels, the 'acceptable' squirrels, though less than a hundred years ago they too were slaughtered on the basis that they damaged forests. Grey squirrels are too often convenient scapegoats, avoiding the need to consider that maybe deforestation had anything to do with the loss of red squirrels or that the persecution of predators might be why there are so many greys. On the latter the latest research suggests that grey squirrel numbers are reduced by the spread of pine martens, now a protected species, though shooting interests and gamekeepers often argue that it shouldn't be. That's how nature works, of course.

Now, I like red squirrels, they're delightful. They visit the feeders in our garden daily and I grew up seeing them in the Formby pinewoods, one of the few areas in England where they've managed to cling on ('pinewoods' may be the key here, as red squirrels much prefer conifers), and I would hate them to die out. It may be that some culling of grey squirrels is needed in those areas where they're encroaching on red squirrels' territory to prevent the spread of a disease fatal to red squirrels, just as culling of deer is needed to allow forests to regenerate. But it should be done only where absolutely necessary, and the greys shouldn't be treated as the 'wrong' sort of wildlife.

This brings up the question of native and non-native. A plant or creature is generally regarded as native or indigenous, the scientific term, if it's present without being introduced by humans. In the case of Scotland, that means having arriving before the land connection with mainland Europe disappeared under the sea some 8,200 years ago. That makes many familiar species non-native. Rabbits were introduced by the Romans, pheasants may have been too, but were certainly established by the fifteenth century, brown hares were brought by Iron Age people, sycamore arrived in the Middle Ages, and European larch in the seventeenth century. All of these and many more, including of course Sitka spruce, have settled well and become integral parts of our natural history.

Dividing species into native and non-native carries the danger of being judgemental. Native good, non-native bad. Natives belong, non-natives don't. The latter, it's often suggested, cause problems, implying the former doesn't. In fact, it's an imbalance in biodiversity, generally caused by humans, behind most difficulties with wildlife. The biggest impediments to the regeneration of forests in Scotland are red and roe deer, both native species. The problem is due to the extermination of predators, not the nature of the deer. The dislike of Sitka spruce is due to the plantation system, not the nature of the tree itself.

The vehemence with which 'non-native' species are sometimes attacked can be disturbingly like racism. 'Invasive', 'alien', 'non-native' are not neutral terms to most people. They imply something or someone that shouldn't be here and that is in some way inferior. Sometimes the usage is alarmingly similar to that used about human immigrants. Rather than being used selectively about the few introduced species that can cause serious problems the words are too often applied generally, just as racist terms can be used to damn all immigrants. That most introduced species cause no problems is ignored as is the fact that immigrants contribute much to society.

Like society, nature is not static. The wild places of the future won't be like those of the past. They will include species first brought here by people, and that should be accepted as positive. Brown hares boxing in a meadow and self-seeded larch trees growing on a crag are part of our nature, and few people would question this. That should apply to everything. There are no good or bad species. Not even midges, though that can be hard to accept when they're driving you crazy.

I'd now been following the Watershed for forty-five days and 850 km. The walk had become my way of life, one of the great joys I find in long-distance walking. This was what I did, this was my day-to-day existence, not an escape from it. I knew though, that I was much closer to the finish than the start. The Southern Uplands felt a long time ago and a long way away. The Flow Country and Duncansby Head were within touching distance. Soon I would have walked the spine of Scotland, the country that was my home, a country I loved.

Those thoughts required contemplation. I'd never been patriotic or nationalistic. I really like the address John Muir wrote in his notebook – 'John Muir, Earth-planet, Universe'. England was simply where I was born. I was aware how privileged I was, how being a white man from one of the richest countries in the world gave me advantages and that it was easy to take those for granted and be unaware of them. But I never felt proud to be English or that England was anywhere special. It was just what I was and where I was. So why did I now feel the way I did about Scotland? How had that happened?

The last question was more easily answered. Slowly and gradually. Noticing little things that began to annoy me, usually casual errors regarding Scotland made by those outwith the country. Assumptions that made me feel defensive. Criticism that came to seem personal. This was my country being maligned. I was beginning to identify with Scotland in a way I never had with England. As to the UK or Britain that had always seemed a political construct about which I had no feelings.

Devolution was a big topic when I moved to Scotland and I followed the debate with interest. Changing the means of government had never seemed a possibility in England. There was a parliament and government in faraway London and every four or five years it could be changed. That was it, really. Other political activity, the sort I took part in, consisted of meetings, demonstrations, arguments in pubs. Affecting the London government never seemed very likely. Devolution really was a chance to make something actually change though. A parliament in Edinburgh able to make decisions on matters important to Scotland but barely a concern in London. I'd always believed in decentralisation anyway, in keeping seats of power small and as answerable as possible. Idealistically I'm a left-wing anarchist, a believer in networks of equals rather than pyramids of power and that decision-making and political power should be as close to the people as possible. There's an interesting website called *The Political Compass* (https://politicalcompass.org/) where you can answer a series of questions that then position you on a square with left/right and authoritarian/libertarian axes. I'm towards the bottom left corner – left wing and libertarian (which is very different from right-wing libertarianism). Devolution was always going to appeal to me. I felt it was more than my already existing long-held beliefs that made me excited by the idea though. I felt strongly that Scotland should have a parliament.

The next step of course was for Scotland to have a government independent of Westminster, for Scotland to no longer be part of the United Kingdom or else to be part of a federal UK where each part was truly equal rather than the present system where one country – England – was so much bigger that it easily dominated the other three. The chance to vote for this came in another referendum, seventeen years after the devolution one. I'd known for some time that I'd vote for independence when the opportunity arose. This time I took out a postal vote – I wasn't risking not being able to vote again as with the devolution referendum. As it was, I was on Harris leading a group up the island's highest hill, Clisham, for the Harris Mountain Festival on the day of the vote. This time I was on the losing side. Scotland voted to stay in the UK. I was disappointed but not surprised. There would, I was sure, be another chance.

That referendum was a year away as I walked the Watershed, a walk that was crystallising how I felt about Scotland and how important it was to me. Many people were surprised at my views – 'but you're English', they said, as though that meant I had no choice in the matter. I was even accused of being a traitor, of betraying the English race, as if that existed and was one homogenous whole, as if the English, the Scots or any people defined by country were somehow completely distinct from any other people. DNA shows this isn't so and there are many people who thought their ancestry was 'pure' who've been shocked to discover they have forebears from places they don't want to be connected with.

I have had my own DNA analysed. The results came out as 66 per cent English, 20 per cent Celtic, 6 per cent Scandinavian and 8 per cent from elsewhere in Europe. I wasn't surprised. My mother had traced her family back to the 1700s and they all came from in and around Rossendale in north-east Lancashire with a preponderance of Hargreaves, Haworths and Walmsleys, and jobs as tenant farmers and labourers. On my father's side I'd been told I had an Irish great-grandfather with the surname Martin, which was why this was my middle name as it was my father's. Research showed that was untrue, the Martin being an alias of my grandfather who was in the army by that name as well as Townsend. Why I don't know, as army records show they knew him under both names and it was hardly a secret. I do have an Irish connection further back though. Townsend/Martin's mother, Catherine Bridget Macdonald, was the daughter of emigrants from Ireland to London. That probably explains the 20 per cent Celt. As to the Scandinavian link, well, the chances are everyone with British ancestry going back a long way has some DNA from that area. And a Scandinavian link doesn't necessarily mean a Viking one, appealing and romantic though that would be. Amongst the Germanic tribes who invaded Britain after the Romans left, the Jutes and the Angles had their origins in Denmark.

DNA tests like this, even though only estimates, are valuable for showing that we are all mixtures of past peoples. At some point all our ancestors arrived here from elsewhere. Whether this was 1,000, 100, 10 or just one year ago doesn't matter. What's important is to feel at home where you settle and to be welcomed. In distance I'd not moved far from northern England to the Scottish Highlands, but I had moved somewhere sufficiently different that I needed to learn about it and to be aware it would take a little while to feel at home. On the Watershed walk I did. I identified with the land, the people, the country, and knew that would never leave me.

Solo long-distance walking gives time for such thoughts, especially in the evenings, sitting or lying in camp. I find this very enriching, and it's one reason I don't take the maximum mileage, least time in camp, fastest time approach. I can't imagine enjoying a walk where I walk non-stop all day, camp at the last minute, fall asleep then repeat the next day and the next and the next. I can admire people who set records by doing this but it's not for me. I think I'd miss so much. I also suspect that I'd give up pretty quickly.

Back on the Watershed, dawn came with a thick mist enveloping the tent and a gusty wind. It had rained overnight and the air was damp and chilly. Gradually the mist rose above camp and a hazy landscape appeared. The summit of Seana Bhraigh was in the cloud as I crossed it. Looking back as I started the long descent of its gentle curving western ridge I could just see the top and beyond it the much more distinctive pinnacle called Creag an Duine – the crag of the man. Out to the north-west lay the long line of ragged Coigach and Assynt hills, dark grey silhouettes against the paler grey sky.

The Watershed headed north-west into in an area known as Rhidorrich – the dark hill slope – which Peter Wright describes as 'a strange and beautiful place, a world apart'. I certainly felt an air of emptiness and quiet here. It's not an area much visited by hillwalkers, few tops reach even 500 metres, but it does have wide-ranging views over land and sea and a subtle beauty. There were many flowers, birches in craggy gorges, a spread of purple heather. A herd of deer watched me warily. Ducks sailed across lochans, and once I heard angry shrieking and looked up to see a peregrine falcon twisting and turning above a crag where I guessed it had a nest, a glorious sight.

The ground was boggy. Looking for somewhere drier I deviated a little from the Watershed to camp above the cluster of ponds called the Clar Lochan, in the midst of a vast sea of green stretching out in every direction. Only in the far distance were there any distinct mountains. This was a rolling gentle land yet one with a feeling of real wildness, albeit grazed heavily by deer.

I crossed Rhidorrich and the similar terrain of the Cromalt Hills on a day of strong winds and myriad cloud patterns, constantly changing and shifting: layers of clouds bright and dark, a wonderful sky. The wind and cloud brought rain, however, and it was falling steadily when I made camp. As the day went on, the wind strengthened. On one top I recorded gusts of 35mph. The altitude was only 254 metres. This was concerning as the next day I hoped to climb the last Munro on the Watershed, 987-metre Conival. Out to the west the skyline, a line of dark silhouettes, rose and fell in the cloud. The familiar dramatic shapes of Ben Mor Coigach, Suilven and Canisp came and went. The sky was alive with layers of clouds, the lowest fast-moving and dark, above it a paler slower moving band, and above that still white clouds and occasional patches of blue. To the north the Conival and Ben More Assynt hills stayed beneath a solid blanket of dark grey that never moved. Just one of the higher hills was in view – spiky An Teallach. The sense of space and wildness was almost overpowering. There was nothing but lochan and burn-dotted moorland stretching over vast distances to those far off hills. Lonely and remote.

There were no paths, but the walking was easy. That was due to the deer, of which I saw many, including one herd of over a hundred. The ground was carved up and well-bitten, with only very low vegetation. Wild, yes, but an over-used landscape. The highest Cromalt top is called, appropriately, Meall a'Bhuirich Rapaig, the hill of the bellowing stags.

The low undramatic, gentle, Cromalt Hills stretch westwards some 8 km from the Watershed to finish at one of the most significant geological features in the Highlands: the Moine Thrust. The long fault line is the reason the scenery to the west is so different to that here. At Knockan Crag, a cliff at the western end of the Cromalt Hills above the A835, there's a visitor centre and some signed trails that explain the Moine Thrust and how its discovery changed geology in the 1880s and 1890s. Before then, the rocks here were a puzzle as billion-year-old Moine Schists lay over 500-million-year-old Cambrian limestone which couldn't be explained by the accepted idea that rock strata were laid down in chronological order, new rocks over old. It was two geologists working in the area, Benjamin Peach and John Horne, who solved the puzzle, working out that over millennia the forces of the earth had pushed older rocks over new ones, creating a low-angle fault line or thrust. At Knockan Crag this can be seen clearly, and you can even put your hand over the 500-million-year gap between the two types of rock. The area from Knockan Crag to Cape Wrath is now the North West Highlands Geopark. All of this lies west of the Watershed from which just those strange-shaped Assynt hills show the geological change.

The last Cromalt Hill on the Watershed is Cnoc na Glas Choille, appropriately named as it means hill of the green forest, and below it lie the conifer plantations that line the A837 road. It will have been different, more natural woods that gave it the name. From this top I descended into the trees and a mix of old tracks and rides to the forest fence and a big metal gate that I climbed to reach the A837. The road and the track I took back into the woods were bright with flowers, especially buttercups but also clover and lesser stitchwort. Away from the verges and beyond a drainage ditch, it was bogland with cotton grass and tormentil. I guessed the strip of land next to the roads was better-drained and so had different vegetation. There were roe deer in the forest. I saw several and heard them calling.

That evening I camped in an open area in the forest, abandoning plans to go further onto open hillside because of the strong gusty wind which, even here, occasionally buffeted the Trailstar. On every side were conifers. I hadn't camped somewhere like this for many weeks and it brought back memories of the Southern Uplands. I realised I was beginning to adjust to the idea of finishing the walk and was starting to review the whole experience and see how it all fitted together. This is a slow process, a gradual winding down, that would now be with me to the end.

The rain woke me several times during the night, lashing against the nylon, but by the time I was having breakfast it had stopped and there was a touch of brightness in the sky and some small patches of blue. The clouds were still moving fast and were very low, with stray grey tendrils not far above the treetops in which the wind roared. There were slugs everywhere. Big black ones on the grasses and smaller brown ones that liked crawling up the mesh of the inner tent. There were many frog hoppers too, little brown bugs whose larvae are found in the tiny balls of white froth known as cuckoo spit and which can jump amazingly high. And jumping they were too, bouncing round as if on a trampoline. Thankfully there were no midges, though in calm weather I imagine they'd be appalling in such a damp sheltered place.

While I watched the little creatures, I considered what to do. Just to the north lay the last long high-level stretch of the Watershed, on it the northernmost Watershed Munro, Conival. I really, really wanted to climb it, but in this wind? 'Leave decision to the last minute', I wrote. I did and went upwards, desire overcoming discretion as the wind hadn't lessened and it was now raining heavily again. Once out of the trees the wind really battered me and walking became difficult. At times I had to lean on my trekking poles and brace myself to avoid being blown over. I struggled to the edge of the cloud and checked my altimeter: 400 metres. I probably wouldn't be able to stand higher up and there was much rocky terrain to cross. Discretion reasserted itself. I would not go on. Reluctant to abandon the Watershed I hesitated, but this was not weather to stand around in while thinking what to do. I knew really the decision had been made. Turning away I descended to the River Oykell and headed for a bridge marked on the map.

It wasn't there, and the river was a white torrent! I headed upstream and eventually found a wider, slower section where I could make a rather unnerving knee-deep ford, the first of three I would make that day. I started out on a stony boggy footpath, which eventually became a fairly new-looking rough and ugly bulldozed track – the map still showed a footpath – that ran below the east side of the Ben More Assynt-Conival massif. There were recent-looking vehicle, horse and boot prints on the track but I met no-one; unsurprising in the storm.

Despite the weather and the ugly track, I found the landscape exhilarating: a really wild tangle of huge boulders, deep-looking bogs, thrashing burns, and many waterfalls with steep mountainsides rising into dark clouds as a backdrop. It felt elemental. I camped beside big Gorm Loch Mor only a kilometre or so from the Watershed. The ground was mostly sodden, and it took me a while to find a dryish, flattish knoll that was sheltered from at least some of the wind. Gusts occasionally roared in and shook the Trailstar, but a touch of pink in the low clouds pouring across the sky gave me hope of better weather.

Early the next day it appeared that wasn't to be. I woke to fine grey sheets of heavy rain sweeping over the landscape from the even faster-moving clouds. I lay watching the storm and realised that I didn't mind, that I was happy to be here. I thought how good it was to wake so close to the earth, to open my eyes and see grass and heather a few inches away and then to raise my head and see rocks and hills. This world was beautiful, even in the rain.

By the time I was packing up the rain had stopped and the wind was easing. There were hints of sunshine and, after another knee-deep ford I headed back to the Watershed and rugged walking through a rough country of boulders, bogs, burns, lochans, knolls and terraces to a final climb to Beinn Leoid, a 792-metre Corbett. On the summit I revelled in the views. Ben More Assynt and Conival, now to the south, were free of cloud. The tops of Quinag, Foinaven and Arkle, their shapes as distinctive as their names, were just hidden.

To the east I could see a figure approaching, a tall thin young man with a big pack. I guessed who it must be. Peter Wright had told me recently that a walker called David Edgar had set off to walk south along the Watershed of Scotland and England a few weeks earlier, and I'd reckoned that we should pass each other around here. I'd hoped we'd meet though I knew we could easily miss each other in the mist or on lower storm-avoiding routes. For the one and only time on the walk I had a fellow long-distance Watershed walker to talk with.

David told me that he reckoned Dunnet Head, the most northerly point on the mainland and well to the west of Duncansby Head, was where the Watershed started so he was walking from there to Dover. His intention was to follow the Watershed exactly and walk to and from all supply points, the first one of which was Ullapool. This was his twelfth day, so he'd set off with a pack heavy with food. He was carrying print-out maps of the whole route too, a big load of paper. I wondered how he'd get on as he didn't know the Highlands and had reckoned the hill he'd just come over, Meallan a'Chuail, was 'a bit rocky'.

Unfortunately, David was forced to stop his walk at Ben Alder due to a knee injury, but didn't abandon the Watershed altogether, returning in 2016 and 2018 to undertake sections. His progress can be followed on his blog at www.loughrigg. org. It was fascinating to meet him. I hadn't expected to meet any other Watershed walkers. On some long-distance routes there are many others, and a big part of the experience is sharing it with them. The West Highland Way is like that as are the Appalachian and Pacific Crest Trails in the USA, both over 2,000 miles long. These are routes where you can walk with others every day and meet up in camps and town stops, if that's what you want. Every year there's a community of thru-hikers, as they're called, on the move. There are organised gatherings when most people start and events along the way. In the USA long-distance hikers often have trail names, chosen by other hikers or themselves. These can be weird and wonderful. Never having done one of these sociable trails (I walked the Pacific Crest Trail long before it became popular), I've managed to avoid having a trail name (which may or may not be a good thing!). Some people go on using their trail name long after the walk is over. Trail names have never caught on in Britain, but the sociability has and the remaining in contact with others met along the way for years afterwards. Hike a long-distance route and, if you wish, you can become part of a long-distance hiking community that is defined by the activity not by location, a community where what you do outside of hiking is irrelevant. Real life is on the trail.

This desire to share the experience is very powerful. Talking to someone who has done the same walk is different to talking to someone, even another long-distance walker, who hasn't. I realised this talking to David. Even though my walk was near the end and his much longer one had only just begun, our shared goal and interest in the Watershed gave us an understanding I hadn't had with anyone else I'd met. Indeed, I doubt many of the other walkers even knew they were on the Watershed.

Knowing this shared experience was important to many, one of my favourite outdoor writers, Hamish Brown, the first man to climb all the Munros in one continuous walk, came up with the idea of a challenge coast-to-coast walk across the Highlands that would take place at the same time each year. He knew that people enjoyed routes like the West Highland Way and the Pennine Way in part because of the shared experience, but he wanted something where the participants plan and navigate their own routes but which wasn't competitive like mountain orienteering events. Backed by *The Great Outdoors* magazine, Hamish's challenge was launched in 1980, initially as The Ultimate Challenge, after an equipment sponsor but later changed to The Great Outdoors Challenge (TGOC). It has proved phenomenally successful, with many people returning to it year after year. I was on the first and have done fifteen so far. I do enjoy the camaraderie at the finish in Montrose where tales are swapped and plans made for the future but I'm quite happy to avoid the big social gatherings during the walk that are often arranged in advance (Braemar has a certain notoriety!). If I meet other Challengers along the way that's good but I don't do the walk to meet people. Meeting David pleased me greatly, but if I'd been meeting Watershed walkers every day I'd have felt it was too popular.

This day was one for meetings though. Two day-walkers arrived on Beinn Leiod as I was chatting to David and then three more on the next summit, Meallan a'Chuail. I hadn't seen so many people for many days. As I left the last summit the sky was clouding over again and the wind picking up. One of the walkers on Beinn Leiod said the forecast was poor for the next day but that the weather was then meant to improve. I followed the Watershed down to the A838 where I met two more walkers, long-distance ones this time. Dave and Joy were walking from their home in Portsmouth to Cape Wrath via roads and tracks.

Camp that night was on boggy moorland not far from the road. Tomorrow I would cross the last high hill on the Watershed, Ben Hee, a Corbett, and leave the Highlands for the Flow Country. The last section of the walk was approaching. Deer were browsing not far from camp. I'd seen many more during the day. The orange spikes of bog asphodel, now very familiar cotton grass, and bushy bog myrtle grew round the Trailstar. The last is said to be a repellent against midges. I didn't need any. The wind was enough. Reflecting on the walk through the Highlands I realised I hadn't been bothered by midges much at all. A month's summer camping and barely any midges! That was a first I didn't expect to repeat.

Heavy rain and a strong blustery wind woke me early. Looking out I saw thick clouds low on the hills. The Highlands didn't look like they were going to let me go easily. They didn't. Another very wet and windy day ensued. I spent much of it in cloud, plodding over boggy slopes, losing all sense of time and seeing little. The final climb to the summit of Ben Hee seemed to go on forever, the horizon always just ahead, always another slope. The storm strengthened, and it was cold enough when I stopped on the top to need a hat and warm top. Ben Hee means fairy hill. Today the fairies seemed in a bad mood and not to want me there.

Whilst tedious the ascent was easy, just a walk up feature-less grassy slopes. The descent wasn't. I quickly found myself going down a very steep tangle of crags and gullies. Peter Wright says it 'requires care'. In this storm I felt that was an understatement. I found it very scary, the wet rocks slick and treacherous, the world below me falling away into nothing-ness. The rock architecture was dramatic and imposing but I wasn't in the mood to really appreciate it. After several attempts I decided retreat was sensible and followed the edge of the crags in search of an easier way down. I passed a rock bergschrund, a huge gash where a massive section of moun-tainside was pulling away. Eventually steep but non-rocky slopes led down to Loch Coire na Saidhe Duibhe. A track took me back to the Watershed only a few hundred metres from where I'd been an hour or more before but now below the crags rather than above them.

I was now on the edge of the mountains though I couldn't see this as I was still in the mist. The Watershed turns south here for several km before finally departing the hills for the Flow Country. I had one last camp in the stormy mountains. Tomorrow I would leave the hills.

7

THE FLOW COUNTRY

The walk was changing but there was no sign of that yet. Just another stormy night in the mountains. I was woken by a fierce wind shaking the Trailstar and then, a few hours later, after the wind had eased and I'd fallen back to sleep, by heavy rain hammering loudly on the nylon just above my head. Over breakfast I watched buttercups and long grasses waving in the wind and listened to the trickle of the nearby burn. I was camped on stony ground, probably once part of the streambed or formed by a gravel outwash. I had needed rocks to pound in the pegs.

The rain stopped but low clouds were still sweeping across the hills when I set off. I wandered south over a couple of low hills then the world opened up and I could see a vast cotton-grass-covered expanse of green, dotted with shining burns and pools stretching out in front of me. The start of the Flow Country, a huge area of peatbogs and dark pools, known as dubh lochain – black lochans – that stretched out east almost to the coast. Covering around 400 square km it's the largest area of blanket bog in Europe and one of the most extensive in the world. The flows, as the areas of bog are called, form in cool areas with high rainfall where drainage is poor, and the soil is low in nutrients.

Sphagnum moss thrives in these conditions and is their main plant. When it dies it forms mats of waterlogged vegetation that, over thousands of years, are compressed to form peat, a natural sponge that can absorb many times its weight of water. On the surface as well as sphagnum, of which there are many species, other bog plants grow: such as cotton grass and insectivorous sundew and butterwort. Under them lies the peat, in places 10 metres thick.

In some areas the first peat began to form after the last ice age, around 10,000 years ago. Other places were lightly wooded and only began to turn to peatbog 7,000 years ago as the climate became wetter and colder. Although from a distance the land looks flat this isn't so; there are many low ridges and little hills, often called cnocs – knolls – and there are higher hills in places.

The Flow Country may not have the dramatic grandeur of the high mountains, but it does have a great sense of space, a seemingly endless world stretching out to distant horizons. The peatland is also very important for its natural history and as a carbon sink. Because it doesn't decay, the dead plant matter that makes up the peat doesn't release its carbon but stores it. If the peat is damaged or dried out this carbon can be released into the atmosphere as carbon dioxide, adding to global warming. As the Flow Country holds more than twice as much carbon as all of Britain's forests, which if released would be equivalent to one hundred years of Britain's fossil fuel emissions, it's important that it's preserved.

The Flow Country isn't suitable for agriculture and was mostly left unspoilt until the 1960s and 1970s when tax incentives led to commercial conifer forests being planted in some areas, damaging the peat with deep ploughing and draining. The people funding the planting were from far away and had no concerns for the Flow Country; they were just interested in offsetting their investment against tax. This led to a huge conservation struggle as it became apparent just how severe the damage was, which eventually led to the law being changed so investing in distant forests was no longer attractive. By then it was also becoming apparent that trees planted on blanket bogs wouldn't produce timber worth much anyway.

Since 1994 a coalition called *Flows for the Future*, led by the RSPB, and including the Forestry Commission, Scottish Natural Heritage, Plantlife and private land owners, has been working together to remove the forests and restore the peatlands by felling the trees, filling the deep ploughed furrows and blocking drains. Slowly the damaged land is recovering though it's a lengthy process.

The area is also very important for wildlife, especially birds. Golden plover, greenshank, dunlin, greylag geese, and red-throated and black-throated divers nest in the bogs. Hen harriers, merlins and short-eared owls hunt over them.

The Flow Country, which I had never visited before, my Land's End to John o'Groats walk having taken me along the coast, sounded wonderful – for birdwatching and plant study. But walking? I wasn't so sure. Days wandering through bogs trying not to fall in pools or get stuck in deep peat didn't sound appealing. I worried about finding dry places to camp and even more about how horrendous the midges would be. Peter Wright's words in *Ribbon of Wildness* only deepened my concerns – 'danger lurks . . . even for the experienced', he wrote, before giving advice on how to walk on quaking peat bogs and saying, 'with any luck, your feet won't sink far'. This was not reassuring. Now I was here I did wonder if I should have chosen to head for Cape Wrath and stayed in the mountains. Peter Wright had convinced me Duncansby Head was the end of the Watershed though. I did want to link the two ends in a continuous walk. Going to Cape Wrath would have felt wrong. And anyway, whatever would I have said to Peter?

I needn't have worried. The experience was to be as far from the one I expected as possible. I found this out as soon as I ventured onto the first flow and headed across it to Cnoc an Alaskie. Peter Wright says that this is a 'terrain of rampant peat hags and quaking bogs' and 'that there is a trig point here is remarkable'. So, I was surprised when I ambled across dry ground to the latter. There were dark pools and areas of soft mud but most of the terrain was not just dry but crisp, crackling underfoot. My shoes, wet for many days, began to dry out. The wind was still strong, but the sky was clear and the sun shone. I looked back. A dark cloud hung over Ben Hee. Out on the moss and beside the trickling burns waders scuttled. I heard them before I saw them – the trilling calls of dunlin with their distinctive black breasts, the thin piping of the familiar common sandpiper, soon spotted running fast on its clockwork-like legs. There was some less attractive wildlife too. Clegs, those big flies that can give a painful bite, were rather prolific, constantly buzzing round looking for flesh to nibble, Swatting them wasn't difficult, but they did detract from the enjoyment of the walk at times.

I left this first surprisingly dry flow for the A836 road and the cosy little Crask Inn, which has served travellers on this lonely road since 1815. The name comes from A Chrasaig, which means the crossing, chosen, I assume, because it lies close to the Watershed and the high point on this lonely road. I'd hoped it would be open and would have food, but I hadn't planned on it as on one previous visit it had been shut. I didn't want that disappointment again. This time it was open though, and extremely busy, which surprised me as it's arguably Scotland's most remote inn, some 14 km from the tiny village of Altnaharra, and over 23 km from Lairg, the nearest little town. It turned out that this was a monthly church gathering and was just ending. There were plates of sandwiches, cakes and scones. 'Help yourself', I was told, 'They're free'. I did. This was most welcome and along with several bars of chocolate I purchased would save me a day's food. Maybe I could make it to Duncansby Head without a diversion.

The Crask Inn had no phone signal but a good Facebook connection. David Edgar had said he was posting updates on his Facebook page. I had a look. He described the previous day's traverse of Conival and Breabag as 'unremittingly grim', just like my day on Ben Hee then, though the storm must have been even worse on those higher hills. In the inn I was told that it had been hot and dry for many weeks here, one of the sunniest summers in memory. As I was to learn, this had been true for most of Scotland. Only along the west coast and a little way inland had it been wet and windy. Just where I'd been. If only the Watershed had been further east!

Although tempted by a pint of beer I decided that alcohol and hot sunshine and bog walking didn't really mix and it was far too early to stop for the day, so I stuck to ginger beer and coffee. The owners were friendly and I was tempted to stay longer chatting. The finish of the walk was pulling me on though, the first time I'd felt that. Until now Duncansby Head had been too far off to really think about. Now I started to have a familiar feeling, a slight concern that something might stop me finishing. Completing the walk had been an abstract aim but not something I'd really thought about before. I'd wanted to enjoy the day-to-day experience and just see how far I got. Now I was close I felt that reaching the finish was important. I was also looking ahead, beyond the walk, to life back home, to life where I didn't pack up my belongings and walk every day. Part of my mind was moving outside this backpacking existence and preparing for it to end. I find this winding down process valuable, but it does distract a little from the last days of a walk. Long-distance walkers often report that things are difficult after a walk, that they can't settle back into their old life. I'd solved that, in a way, years before by making walking and the outdoors and writing about them my way of life. There was always another long walk to come. Even so, I knew the abrupt change from hiking to home could be disorientating. Letting my mind wander to the future was a way of easing out of the walk. These thoughts and feelings would grow in the next few days.

My last visit to the Crask Inn had been to celebrate the end of someone else's long walk, a very different gathering to the one I'd just walked into. A group of us had accompanied Steve Perry to the summit of Ben Hope at the end of his continuous winter walk over all the Munros, the first time this had been done, and an extremely tough and impressive venture. Appropriately it was snowing on the summit. Afterwards we'd repaired to the Crask to party.

Before I left the Crask another long-distance traveller arrived, a weary and hot-looking cyclist from Bournemouth who was on the 15th day of a Land's End to John o'Groats ride. He planned to finish in two more days and said he was enjoying the trip, but the headwinds had been bad since he reached Scotland. I can admire long-distance cyclists but it's not something I'd like to do. Not that I have anything against cycling. I enjoy riding round the quiet roads and tracks where I live, and I'd used a bike on long road sections on my round of the Munros and Tops. It's the traffic I'd find a problem. The noise, the smell, the danger. Roads and tracks with hardly any vehicles would be fine.

From the A836 the Watershed appears to be heading for the mountains again as it starts up the south-western slopes of big bulky Ben Klibreck, the most northerly Munro but one. However, it turns away long before the summit and drops to the Bealach Easach. From here I had a splendid view down to Loch a'Bhealaich and Loch Choire in the glen below. I could see a good path running down to the lochs. Kai, one of the owners of the Crask Inn, had told me there was an open bothy down there. Feeling tired despite not having had any beer – I suspected the unfamiliar heat – I decided to head down to it. The Watershed traversed the big heathery moorland hills above the lochs. Somehow, they didn't look appealing. I went down to the bothy and was glad I did as it's situated in a beautiful spot on the shores of Loch Choire, which has big curving golden sand beaches that looked lovely in the sunshine. In the evening shafts of sunlight split the clouds that rose high into the western sky and made the dark waters of the loch a shining silver. A sign outside said the bothy was called Choire na Fearna – the corrie of the alders – and there were indeed some alders growing nearby. There were birch woods too, some of them fenced to allow regeneration.

The bothy was small, just a small corrugated iron shed but, inside, the walls were lined with plywood, and there was a table, chairs and a big sleeping platform so it was comfortable enough. This isn't an MBA bothy, but the local estate leaves it open for anyone to use. A notice said it was maintained in memory of Albert Grant, head stalker from 1976 to 2008. The bothy book suggested there were few visitors, unsurprising in such a remote spot, but sadly there was a fair amount of rubbish plus quite a bit of food, some past its use-by date. I packed some of the plastic waste to take with me, it hardly weighed anything, and, as my supplies were running low it being a week since I'd left Ullapool, ate an out-of-date can of soup for supper, rinsing out and flattening the can afterwards to add to my bag of rubbish.

The light was wonderful early the next morning. Thin clouds drifted over Ben Klibreck. The trees and the loch and the sand glowed softly, green and blue and gold. Pied wagtails darted about the loch shore. There was no wind. Idyllic. Except for the midges, which swarmed around me as soon as I stepped outside. I was glad I was in a bothy where it was much easier to have breakfast and pack up than in the Trailstar. The midges set one of the day's themes. That evening I wrote 'a day of distance, sunshine and biting insects. Clegs most of day, sometimes a dozen or more buzzing round, then as sun weakened and breeze dropped clouds of midges forcing fast retreat into inner'.

The day was still enjoyable though, a relaxing day of easy walking, good weather, and much birdlife. Alongside Loch Choire there was a heartening amount of natural woodland, some of it fenced. Mostly birch but also alder, willow, rowan, and holly then, just before ruined Loch Choire Lodge, larch, Scots Pine, beech and cedars appeared – estate woodlands planted to enhance the building's situation. Beyond the loch I came out into the vast expanse of the Flow Country again. To the north I could see the outline of distant Ben Loyal, a fine mountain not far from the coast. This sense of unbroken space, these seemingly endless sightlines, are soon to be broken by a massive windfarm, thirty-nine huge turbines up to 135 metres high, rising out of the peatbogs. Despite opposition from the RSPB, the John Muir Trust and Highland Council, the Scottish Government has given the go-ahead for the damaging Strathy South wind farm to go ahead. I was glad I'd been here to see the unbroken immensity of the Flow Country but I'm sad that this splendour will soon be sullied.

The wind farm will harm wildlife, damage an important habitat, and almost certainly not do anything to mitigate climate change as it will be built on pristine peatland whose carbon stores will be released during its construction. An Aberdeen University study concluded that 'building wind farms on pristine peat is a bad idea for carbon emissions'. The John Muir Trust said, 'this is a landscape of striking natural beauty and international ecological importance . . . we would like to see national investment in the restoration of peatland and other natural habitats in the Flow Country'. That should be the way forward not further despoiling the area with wind farms. The Scottish Government committed millions of pounds to a major programme of peatland restoration a year before it gave the go-ahead for the Strathy South wind farm. Maybe some of that money could be used to remove the wind farm as soon as it's built.

The dry crunchy ground made for fast walking. Sometimes I was on tracks, sometimes cross-country. On one of the former I met two mountain bikers cycling in to a couple of remote hills they wanted to climb. A few vehicles passed me, sending huge clouds of dust into the air, which I saw long before they appeared. It reminded me of walking in the dry areas of the American West. But this was the notoriously wet Flow Country! The many lochs were all a beautiful deep blue. On the open ground there were lapwings, oystercatchers, sandpipers and wagtails. A buzzard sailed overhead. Swallows twisted and turned in the hot air. In the small woods and copses I spotted wrens, chaffinches and blackbirds. There were trenches cut in the peat in places with stacks of peat blocks beside them, drying for burning in hearths and stoves, a tradition going back thousands of years. It's a good fuel. I've burnt it at home and love the smell. Too much peat cutting, especially commercially, often for compost for gardens, can do damage, however. These cuttings were small and, I guess, for local use. Whilst hand-harvesting does a little damage it is on a very small-scale unlike the massive industrial diggings where heavy machinery is used to strip away large areas.

As I approached the Strath of Kildonan with its road and railway I was reminded that this beautiful, lonely and peaceful landscape has a dark and brutal past. Some of the worst excesses of the Clearances happened in the Flow Country in the 1810s when Patrick Sellars, factor for the Duke of Sutherland, evicted people from their homes, burning them down around them if they refused to leave, to make way for sheep. After a woman nearly a hundred years old was left in her house while it was set alight he was charged with murder – she was rescued but died two days later – but found not guilty. Sellars went on to become one of the largest landowners in the area and ran a huge profitable sheep farm. Twenty km of the Watershed runs through it.

I'd seen ruined buildings and shielings throughout the Highlands but there was nothing to say whether these were due to the Clearances or not. In the Strath of Kildonan I came on a sign for Scotland's Clearances Trail with a barcode to scan and details of a phone app that can be used to follow the trail. This has been produced by Timespan, which is based in Helmsdale on the coast to the south. It's a great idea and one I think that could be followed elsewhere to reveal the history of places. Seeing the sign was a sober reminder of what once took place here.

After 40 km, the furthest I'd walked on any day, though it didn't feel like it as there was little ascent, no difficult terrain and I was now pretty fit, I camped near a conifer plantation not far from the Watershed on Knockfin Heights. After gathering twigs for my stove, I sat outside cooking over wood for only the second time on the walk. It was a lovely warm and peaceful evening until the sun set and the midges came out. The midge repellent I'd been carrying since the start was finally getting some use. But then so was the sunscreen.

I woke to a completely clear sky with not even a tiny wisp of cloud. The Trailstar was soaked inside and out but dried fast once the sun rose. I could hear pigeons cooing in the nearby trees. The ground round camp was dotted with tiny eyebright. This pretty delicate flower looks white at a glance but look closely and you can see thin purple stripes on the lobed petals and a yellow spot in the centre.

The next day was one of the hottest yet with no clouds in the sky until late evening. The Knockfin Heights flow, marked as a pool-dotted marsh on the map, was again dry and crunchy. I was getting used to dry feet. Where I could I walked on the bare dusty brown peat between the tussocks of moss and heather as it was smooth and firm. I saw many deer and some greenshanks, the first time I'd seen this wader. Lizards scuttled over the dry ground, frogs hopped in the wetter places. This part of the Flow Country is now the Flows National Nature Reserve, which will hopefully mean it's protected from developments.

All day the views were dominated by the distinctive cone of Morven, the only really prominent hill in Caithness – the name comes from the Gaelic *A' Mhòr Bheinn*, the big hill. I'd drop down into a shallow dip and look up to see just its tip appearing above an otherwise dead straight horizon. At other times I could see the long line of lower hills trailing out from it. Other than Morven the view was one of open space stretching, it felt, to infinity.

I walked with mixed feelings. The end of the walk was only a few days away and my adventure was coming to an end. That made me feel a little sad. I didn't want to finish. At the same time, I felt impatient to do so. The purity of the walk, of knowing that for the foreseeable future I would be walking on every day, was over. Restless, I found it hard to enjoy the here and now. As I knew I would soon stop, part of me wanted to get it over with and start adapting to life after the walk. Slowly I was parting company with it.

With these thoughts in mind a quicker route to the finish began to appeal. I'd missed enough of the actual Watershed now, though I'd never been far from it, that not following it precisely wasn't a major concern. The walk was a success anyway. I'd done what I'd intended to do: the deep aim behind following the Watershed was to spend weeks walking and wild camping, and my walk had been continuous. The map showed an interesting-looking long glen with crags and waterfalls and a path running down it beside the Glutt Water. The Watershed ran over the low hills just above the glen. I decided to take the glen, which made for a lovely walk past the Eas Gluta Waterfall and beside the sparkling river.

The path became a track, passing huge derelict Dalnawillan Lodge, and the Glutt Water became the River Thurso. A sign on the gate at Dalnagachan farm said 'Walkers Welcome'. I wondered how many came here. I had seen no-one bar the two cyclists and the few vehicles. That night I camped on a knoll above the River Thurso with huge flat vistas all around. Open space country broken only by distant wind farms to the east. The hardest part of the day was going down to the river for water as I had to push through dense head-high reeds and grasses.

A strong wind picked up during the night and woke me several times. An east wind, it brought low cloud that almost shrouded my camp. There was just enough coffee left to make a mug for breakfast. Ten days out from Ullapool and my supplies had almost run out, but with just two days' walking left I wasn't bothered about feeling hungry. As the clouds rose and the sun came out I sat and looked at vastness all around. The sense of freedom and space was overwhelming. I was glad I took time to relish being here. It was to be my last camp.

The wind was still gusting when I set off, blowing clouds of dust into the air. The clouds had cleared though and the sun was hot – a third day for sandals and shorts. It was also a day for coming down from the walk and for leaving the Flow Country moors for lowland farmland. That I was separating myself from the walk could be seen in my journal. I wrote far less the last few days.

The morning brought birds, especially raptors. Buzzards wheeled overhead. A long-winged pale grey bird skimmed over the River Thurso and began circling over the moorland. A hen harrier! I was thrilled. This was a bird I'd wanted to see and that I knew frequented the Flow Country. I stood and watched it for many minutes. Hen harriers are graceful and beautiful birds and have become a symbol for conservationists due to their rarity, especially on grouse shooting moors where there should be many more of them. Having been nearly exterminated they are now a protected species but illegal killing still goes on. The story is well-told in Mark Avery's *Inglorious: Conflict in the Uplands*. The RSPB is concerned too that hen harriers, along with other species, will be at risk from the Strathy South wind farm.

Shortly after watching the hen harrier I heard a loud screeching and looked up to see a peregrine falcon zooming by high overhead. The Flow Country was giving me a fine send-off. Twice I saw herons lumbering over the river, their

163

huge wings flapping slowly. Beyond big Loch More the land began to change. The moors faded away. Instead there were fields, bales of hay, cows, walls, and fences. Roads and buildings appeared. Somewhere here I crossed the Watershed as it made a loop north. It had been south of me all day. To the east, low grey mist lay on the horizon, the haar, that cold fog that is blown in off the North Sea by the wind. I joined a minor road and followed it to the village of Watten, my mind on food rather than the route. I found it in the Watten Brown Trout Hotel and a room in the Loch Watten B&B. My last night would be spent indoors. The walk really was coming to an end.

As I made my way through the farmland I thought about my walk, about the Watershed, about its future. I felt happy with the walk. It had been what I wanted, what I needed. I had stuck to my personal rule for long-distance walks and kept it continuous, always returning to the same point if I left it. I knew that over the weeks and months to come the walk would change in my mind. Already the stormy days were beginning to merge together. Certain places and events seemed more real than others. Setting out felt almost like a different walk. The Southern Uplands far away in distance, time and experience. I'd walked the length of the country. The Watershed was, in a sense, part of me now and always would be.

In my mind I could see the line of the Watershed stretching out down the country, all the back to Peel Fell. I could see how it connected all those different places into one continuous whole, Peter Wright's Ribbon of Wildness. It was wild too, mostly, a high line with some of the toughest walking I'd ever done and a feeling of remoteness and space that had surprised me in places, especially in the Central Lowlands, which were the real revelation of the walk.

The Flow Country had surprised me too, due to the dryness, but I knew that here the conditions were temporary and it wasn't usually like this. I doubt you can often walk across it in low-cut shoes and sandals and keep your feet dry. Looking back, I saw the Watershed as a spine that holds the Scottish mainland landscape together. Everything runs from this twisting, turning line of high, wild land. When I think of Scotland now I don't just see the dots of hills or the lines of long-distance paths that go against the grain of the land. I see the Watershed snaking out across the hills, holding it all together.

What happens to the Watershed now concerned me. There's nothing like actually walking somewhere to appreciate it and want to conserve it. That line through the country deserves recognition and care. Much of it is theoretically protected. Peter Wright lists a host of acronyms for designations covering different areas – SSSI, SPA, SAC, NNR, NSA, Ramsar, since joined by Wild Land Areas – going all the way back to 1949, the year I was born, and covering eighty-nine different places along the Watershed. Wright also lists twenty-two agencies and organisations with an active conservation or biodiversity role. None of these bodies or designations even mentions the Watershed though. That it passes through the areas they're concerned with is a coincidence. Each organisation and designation has different concerns but, even so, it seems there are too many with overlapping interests. And only 30 per cent of the Watershed is actually protected.

The key to unifying all these designations for much of the Watershed in the Highlands lies, I think, in the Wild Land Areas, which were announced a year after my walk. The Watershed runs through fourteen of these, covering most of the ground from Loch Lomond to the Flow Country. This gives a common thread for protecting the Watershed in these areas. There are, unsurprisingly, no Wild Land Areas along the Watershed in the Central Lowlands and only one in the Southern Uplands so a different approach needs to be taken here. Scottish Natural Heritage has described every Wild Land Area with its key attributes and qualities. It is to be hoped that the Scottish Government takes conserving these areas seriously.

Now I can see the Watershed as a whole, it seems to me that there should be a single body whose aim is to conserve and promote it. Peter Wright has been working on setting one up since he wrote his book. His Ribbon of Wildness Group has been created 'to develop widespread awareness of the Watershed of Scotland as an irreplaceable National asset for ecology, public enjoyment and well-being . . . and to achieve some form of formal National recognition for this'. I support this wholeheartedly and hope to be working with Peter to achieve it. Long-distance walks change lives and, in this case, it made me aware of the Watershed and aware of the need to conserve it in a way I hadn't felt just by reading about it. Peter's is an ambitious idea and that's great. We need optimism and bold thinking. It can be followed at https://www.ribbonofwildness.co.uk.

Political referendums had played a part in my thoughts during the walk, and one could be said to have had an important part to play. The vote to set up a Scottish Parliament had led to the access legislation that meant I could walk the Watershed without worrying about being thrown off land or told I couldn't camp. My feelings about Scotland had been firmed up by the Scottish Independence Referendum. That this would take place I knew before I set off. The Act confirming it was passed by the Scottish Parliament while I was on the walk, the day I followed the Watershed over Beinn Bheoil in fact. Thinking about how I would vote and why crystallised my feelings that Scotland was home. I was on the losing side that time but having to think about it, which I did during the walk, was valuable.

At the time of the walk proposals for another referendum were going through the UK Parliament, this one on European Union membership. It hadn't impinged on my consciousness so much, but I knew when it took place I'd vote to stay in the EU. Again I was on the losing side and this time the result looked as though it could be detrimental to the conservation of wild places and the Watershed. Just about every environmental, conservation and wildlife organisation called for the UK to stay in the EU because of the importance of EU legislation to their interests. Along the Watershed forty-five places were covered by the EU Habitats Directive and the EU Conservation of Wild Birds Directive. These are important designations and there seems little likelihood they'll be maintained as strongly, if at all, when the UK is no longer in the EU. Alternative protection seems essential, but will it come? Perhaps if Scotland becomes independent and remains in the EU – Scotland did vote decisively to do so. Wanting to leave the UK and stay in the EU may seem contradictory but it isn't. An independent Scotland would have a direct voice in EU affairs unlike at present when it's the UK that does, with its dominance by England.

Escaping politics may seem a reason to go on a long walk, and I certainly didn't think about such matters much of the time. But if we want wild places, a healthy environment, increased biodiversity and a world worth living in, politics can't be ignored. Those decisions made in parliaments far away in big cities can have a profound effect on nature. Campaigning so the voices of those who love wild places and the natural world are heard is essential.

Could the Watershed ever become a long-distance path? I'd thought about this on and off throughout the walk. In the sense of the Southern Upland Way or West Highland Way with waymarks, signposts and an actual path I very much doubt it. The amount of work required, and the cost, would be prohibitive. I could see sections of it being like that though and I certainly think it should be marked at road crossings, though not in wild places, so people know of its existence and what it is. The Watershed is of great geographical significance, yet many people have no idea where it is or when they are on it or crossing it.

My time on the Watershed was almost over. My last day began misty and cool. The haar was stretching its tendrils inland. The coast was just 11 km away, but I'd walk much further to reach it. I passed big Loch Watten – the name means 'lake lake', as Watten is from the Norse Vatn, water – whose banks were rich with creamy meadowsweet, its scent wafting through the air. I reached the Watershed again and followed it for the final time over low moorland, a sudden return to the remoteness and space of the Flow Country.

At an undistinguished gentle hill with a communications mast I paused. In the distance was the sea. I was almost there. The walk was almost over. I felt relieved and sad. From Warth Hill, the last one on the Watershed, I caught my first hazy glimpse of Duncansby Head and its white lighthouse. The descent to the coast took me through some final peatbogs.

The last few km along the cliff tops to Duncansby Head were splendid, a final flourish. The thin mist of the harr hung round the great shattered crags and the big spires and towers of the Stacks of Duncansby. It all felt slightly ethereal and unreal, which fitted my mood exactly.

As I approached the lighthouse a figure waved. Peter Wright had come to meet me. I was pleased to see him but felt empty, drained. I had made it and now it was over. Time to go home. I wrote little in my journal that day. The final line said it all really.

'I now have a picture of the Watershed in my mind'.

BIBLIOGRAPHY

Adams, Douglas, *So Long And Thanks For All The Fish*, Pan 2016

Avery, Mark, *Inglorious: Conflict in the Uplands*, Bloomsbury 2015

Bain, Clifton, *The Ancient Pinewoods of Scotland: A Traveller's Guide*, Sandstone Press 2013

Brown, Hamish, *Hamish's Mountain Walk*, Sandstone Press 2010

Crumley, Jim, *The Last Wolf*, Birlinn 2010

Crumley, Jim, *The Great Wood: The Ancient Forest of Caledon*, Birlinn 2014

Darling, Frank Fraser & J. Morton Boyd, *The Highlands and Islands*, Collins 1964

Drummond, Peter, *Scottish Hill Names: Their Origin and Meaning*, SMT, 2007

Hetherington, David, *The Lynx And Us*, Scotland: The Big Picture 2018

Hewitt, Dave, *Walking the Watershed: The Border to Cape Wrath Along Scotland's Great Divide*, TACit Press 1994

Leopold, Aldo, *A Sand County Almanac and Sketches Here and There*, Oxford University Press 1949

Lindsay, Ann and Syd House, *The Tree Collector: The Life and Explorations of David Douglas*, Aurum Press 2005

MacInnes, Kellan, *Caleb's List: Climbing the Scottish Mountains Visible from Arthur's Seat*, Luath Press 2012

Monbiot, George, *Feral: Rewilding the Land, Sea and Human Life*, Penguin 2014

Murray, W. H., *Mountaineering in Scotland & Undiscovered Scotland*, Baton Wicks 1997

Shepherd, Nan, *The Living Mountain*, Canongate 2011

Stott, Louis, *The Waterfalls of Scotland*, Aberdeen University Press 1987

Wright, Peter, *Ribbon of Wildness: Discovering the Watershed of Scotland*, Luath Press 2010

WINNER OF THE OUTDOOR WRITERS
AND PHOTOGRAPHERS GUILD: OUTDOOR
BOOK OF THE YEAR AWARD 2016

Drawing from more than forty years of experience
as an outdoorsman, Chris Townsend describes the
landscapes and wildlife, the walkers and climbers, and
the authors who have influenced him in this lucid and
beautiful book. Writing from his home in the heart of
the Cairngorms he discusses the wild, its importance
to civilisation and how we cannot do without it.

'Townsend has achieved his aim of inspiring
others with this book.' *The Scots Magazine*

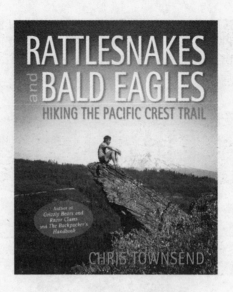

RATTLESNAKES
and BALD EAGLES
HIKING THE PACIFIC CREST TRAIL

Author of
Grizzly Bears and
Razor Clams
and The Backpacker's
Handbook

CHRIS TOWNSEND

The Pacific Crest Trail runs 2,600 miles from
Mexico to Canada through desert, forest and
mountain wildernesses. In *Rattlesnakes and Bald
Eagles* Chris recounts not only his own six-month
walk but also the longer story of the Trail itself,
sharing his ideas and reflections on how the trail is
developing, its future and consequent challenges.

'Chris's books shake you out of lethargy and install
in you that love of the natural world that keeps
us all going.'   Andy Howell, Outdoors Blog

GRIZZLY BEARS AND RAZOR CLAMS
Walking America's Pacific Northwest Trail

Chris Townsend

The story of Chris Townsend's walk along the
1200 mile Pacific Northwest Trail, from the
Rocky Mountains to the Pacific Ocean through
Montana, Idaho and Washington state.

The trail is in its infancy; a mix of signed
footpaths, abandoned trails, dirt roads, animal
tracks and cross-country hikes that made
hiking difficult and sometimes hazardous.

With three national parks – Glacier, North Cascades
and Olympic – along the way, the trail passes through
some of the most magnificent landscapes in the
USA, many of which are pictured in the book in the
author's photographs, all taken during the walk.

www.sandstonepress.com

facebook.com/SandstonePress/

@SandstonePress